General

Ctrl+O	Opens an existing database
Ctrl+S	Saves the active database co
Ctrl+P	Prints the active database
Ctrl+Z *or* Alt+Backspace	Undoes the last action
Ctrl+C	Copies selection to Windows Clipboard
Ctrl+X	Deletes selection and places copy in Clipboard
Ctrl+V *or* Shift+Insert	Pastes in Clipboard contents
Ctrl+F	Carries out a Find operation
Ctrl+H	Carries out a Find-and-Replace operation
Ctrl+:	Inserts current time
Ctrl+;	Inserts current date
Ctrl+Alt+Spacebar	Inserts default value for a field (if applicable)
Ctrl+'	Inserts the value from the same field in the previous record
Ctrl++	Inserts a new blank record
Ctrl+-	Deletes the active record

In datasheets

F2	Switches between Edit and Navigation modes
Tab	Moves to next field
Shift+Tab	Moves to previous field
End	Moves to last field in active record
Home	Moves to first field in active record
Down cursor	Moves to the active field in the next record
Up cursor	Moves to the active field in the previous record
Ctrl+End	Moves to the last field in the last record
Ctrl+Home	Moves to the first field in the first record
Ctrl+W	Closes the active database
Alt+F4	Closes Access

About the Series

In easy steps series is developed for time-sensitive people who want results fast. It is designed for quick, easy and effortless learning. Titles include:

General	Microsoft Outlook	QuickBooks UK
Networking with Windows 98	Microsoft Project	Quicken UK
Networking (with Windows 95)	Microsoft Works	Sage Instant Accounting
PCs	PowerPoint 2000	Sage Line 50
Shareware	PowerPoint	Sage Sterling for Windows
Upgrading Your PC	SmartSuite (Millennium)	**Internet**
Year 2000	Word 2000	AOL UK
Operating Systems	Word 97	CompuServe UK
Linux	Word	FrontPage 2000
Psion 5	WordPerfect	FrontPage
Unix	Word Pro	HTML
Windows 98	**Graphics and DTP**	Internet Culture
Windows 98 - Special Edition	AutoCAD 14	Internet Directory UK
Windows 95	AutoCAD LT	Internet Explorer 4
Windows CE	CorelDRAW	Internet UK
Windows NT	Design and Typography	MSN UK
Main Office Applications	Illustrator	Netscape Communicator
Access 2000	PageMaker	Web Page Design
Access	PagePlus	**Development Tools**
Excel 2000	Paint Shop Pro	Java
Excel	Photoshop	Java Applets
Microsoft Office 2000	Publisher	JavaScript
Microsoft Office 97	QuarkXPress	Perl
Microsoft Office	**Accounting and Finance**	Visual Basic
Microsoft Office SBE	Microsoft Money UK	Visual C++

Web: http://www.computerstep.com

Tel: +44 (0)1926 817999   Fax: +44 (0)1926 817005   Email: books@computerstep.com

ACCESS
in easy steps

Stephen Copestake

In easy steps is an imprint of Computer Step
Southfield Road . Southam
Warwickshire CV33 OFB . England

Tel: 01926 817999 Fax: 01926 817005
http://www.computerstep.com

Reprinted 1999, 1998
Second edition published 1997
First edition published 1996

Notice of Liability
Every effort has been made to ensure that this book contains accurate
and current information. However, Computer Step and the author shall
not be liable for any loss or damage suffered by readers as a result of
any information contained herein.

Trademarks
Microsoft® and Windows® are registered trademarks of Microsoft
Corporation. All other trademarks are acknowledged as belonging to
their respective companies.

Printed and bound in the United Kingdom

ISBN 1-874029-78-4

Contents

4   Creating forms   55

5   Viewing and editing data   75

First steps

This chapter gives you the fundamentals of starting Access for the first time, and closing it when you've finished your current session. It provides brief details of ways in which you can customise some of its basic features to your own requirements. You'll learn how to add new buttons to toolbars and (for Access 97 users only) to menus, and how to specify which toolbars display. Finally, you'll also learn to use Access' on-line HELP system, including the animated Office Assistant (or the Answer Wizard, for Access 95 users) which lets you frame questions in the way *you* want.

Chapter One

Covers

Starting Access (1)

You can launch Access in a variety of ways. The following method is perhaps the easiest to use.

Access lets you create a blank database, as here, when you launch it or a database based on a specific template or wizard. (See Chapter 2 for how to use templates and wizards.)

Running Access

Press Ctrl+Esc. Now do the following:

| Click here

2 Click this tab

Re step 2 – Access 95 users should select the *Databases* tab before carrying out steps 3 and 4.

3 Click here

4 Click here

Starting Access (2)

Here, we're concerned with launching Access with a blank database. Now do the following:

Click here

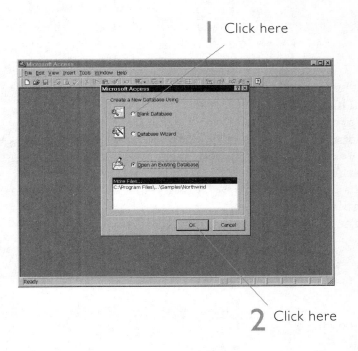

2 Click here

3 Click here; select the drive/folder you want to host the new database

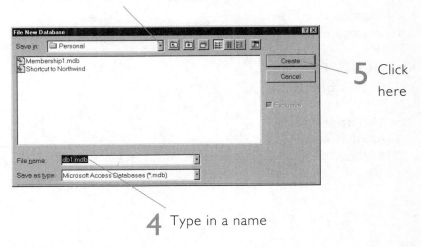

5 Click here

4 Type in a name

Starting Access (3)

There are two further dialogs which have to be negotiated. After step 2 below, Access launches a straightforward database in Datasheet view (this is a way of viewing database data which is strongly reminiscent of spreadsheets – see Chapter 5 for more information). Do the following:

This process creates a very simple database. For how to create a more complex one, see Chapter 2.

Click here

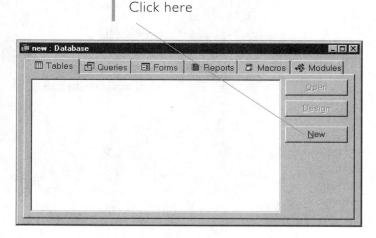

To close down Access, do any of the following:

- **pull down the File menu and click Exit**
- **press Alt+F4**
- **click this button:** ☒ **on the upper far right of the Access Title bar**

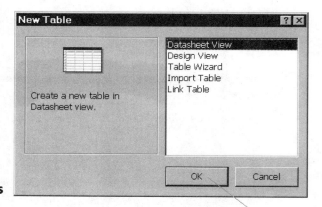

2 Click here

The Access screen

Below is a detailed illustration of a typical Access screen:

Title bar   Menu bar

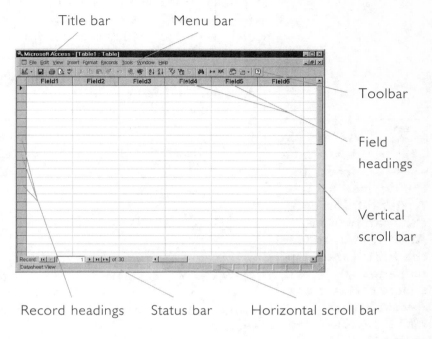

Toolbar

Field headings

Vertical scroll bar

Record headings   Status bar   Horizontal scroll bar

You can also hide or show specific toolbars; see the 'Toolbars (1)' topic on the following page.

Some of these – e.g. the rulers and scroll bars – are standard to all programs which run under Windows. One – the Status bar – can be hidden, if required.

Specifying whether the Status bar displays

Pull down the Tools menu and click Options. Then do the following:

In earlier versions, this dialog was slightly different.

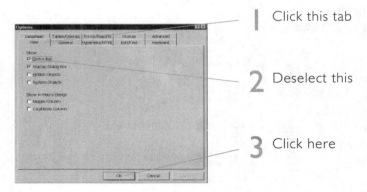

1 Click this tab

2 Deselect this

3 Click here

Toolbars (1)

Toolbars are important components in Access. A toolbar is an on-screen bar which contains shortcut buttons. These symbolise and allow easy access to often-used commands which would normally have to be invoked via one or more menus.

For example, Access' Table Datasheet toolbar lets you:

- save and print documents

- perform copy-and-paste and cut-and-paste operations

- launch Print Preview

- switch to different views

- launch the Office Assistant

by simply clicking the relevant button.

Access 97 provides 22 separate toolbars (Access 95 provides 19). We'll be looking at several of these in more detail as we encounter them. For the moment, some general advice:

Specifying which toolbars are displayed

Pull down the View menu and click Toolbars, Customize. Now do the following:

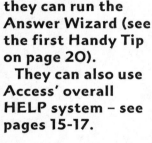

Users of Access 95 don't have access to the Office Assistant; instead, they can run the Answer Wizard (see the first Handy Tip on page 20).
   They can also use Access' overall HELP system – see pages 15-17.

If you're using Access 95, carry out the following procedure instead of steps 1 and 2.
   Pull down the View menu and click Toolbars. In the Toolbars dialog, select the toolbar(s) you want to reveal. Click Close.

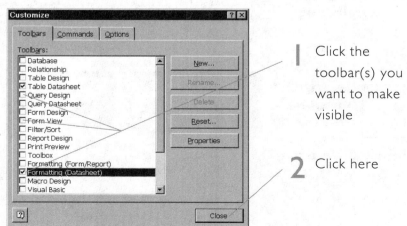

1 Click the toolbar(s) you want to make visible

2 Click here

Toolbars (2)

In versions before 97, these toolbars contain differing numbers of buttons.

Access 97 users can also do the following:
To insert menu buttons into a toolbar, follow step 1. In step 2, click Built-in Menus. In 3 and 4, drag a menu entry onto a toolbar. Finally, follow step 5.
Conversely, to insert a toolbar button into a menu, follow steps 1-4 but drag the button onto the correct location in any *Menu bar* entry. Now follow step 5.

Users of Access 95 should omit step 1.
Additionally, this dialog is slightly different.

Adding buttons to toolbars

By default, the pre-defined toolbars which come with Access have only a comparatively small number of buttons associated with them (for instance, the Table Datasheet toolbar has 23, while the Database toolbar – which you'll probably use frequently – has 17). However, just about all editing operations you can perform from within Access menus can be incorporated (for ease of access) as a button within the toolbar of your choice. The process is convenient and easy to implement.

First make sure the toolbar you want to add one or more buttons to is visible (see the 'Toolbars (1)' topic for how to do this). Move the mouse pointer over the toolbar and right-click once. In the menu which appears, click Customize. Now do the following:

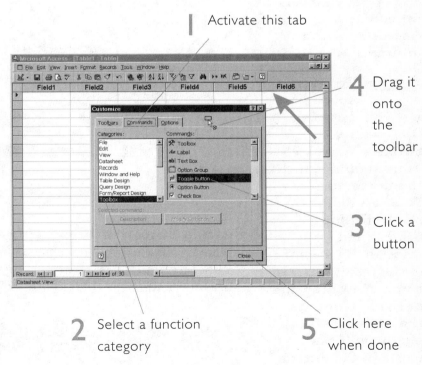

Activate this tab

4 Drag it onto the toolbar

3 Click a button

2 Select a function category

5 Click here when done

Toolbars (3)

Access 97 users can use the Web toolbar to browse through or open any Web documents. For example, click ← to move backwards, → to move forwards. Click Favorites, Add to Favorites to add the current Web page to your list of often-used sites.

   See later chapters for how to use Access 97 with the Internet.

To insert a space between two buttons, Access 95 users should launch the Customize Toolbars dialog by right-clicking a toolbar and selecting Customize in the resultant menu. Now drag one of the buttons to the right or left by almost half the width of the button. Finally, follow step 3.

You can also remove buttons from toolbars, and adjust the intervals between them (by inserting a separator bar if you're using Access 97, or a gap if you're using Access 95).

Deleting toolbar buttons

First make sure the relevant toolbar is visible (see the 'Toolbars (1)' topic for how to do this). Move the mouse pointer over the toolbar and right-click once. In the menu which appears, click Customize. Now do the following:

1 Click a button

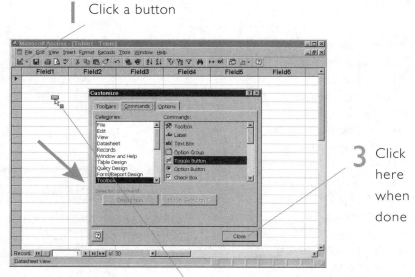

3 Click here when done

2 Drag it off the toolbar

Adjusting button intervals (for Access 97 users)

First, launch the Customize dialog (see above). Right-click the button before which you want the separator inserted. In the menu which launches, click Begin a Group.

Before...

After...

Finally, follow step 3 above.

Using the Access HELP system (1)

HANDY TIP

Users of Access 95 should select Microsoft Access Help Topics in the Help menu.

Access has comprehensive Help facilities:

- Contents (a nested list of topics)

- Index (an alphabetical list of topics)

To generate either of these, pull down the Help menu and choose Contents and Index.

Using Contents

Carry out steps 1 and 2 below:

HANDY TIP

After step 2, Access launches a series of sub-headings. When you find the topic you want information on (prefixed by ⓘ), double-click it. Finally, perform step 3.

Activate this tab

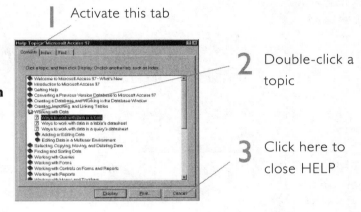

2 Double-click a topic

3 Click here to close HELP

Using Index

Carry out steps 1-3 below (or 4 to close HELP):

HANDY TIP

Both of the dialogs shown here are slightly different in versions before 97.

Activate this tab

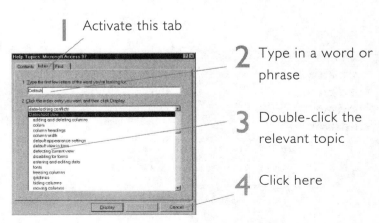

2 Type in a word or phrase

3 Double-click the relevant topic

4 Click here

Using the Access HELP system (2)

When you've used the Contents or Index sections of HELP to pick the topic you want help with, Access displays it as a separate window. Carry out steps 1-3 below, as appropriate:

**Re step 2 –
the Back
button is
greyed out
– and therefore
unavailable – if no
HELP topics were
previously referred
to in the current
session.**

Click here to return to Index or Contents

2 Click here to
return to an earlier
topic (if applicable)

**This is a
magnified
view of a
link – see
step 3.**

3 Click any link (underlined) to
launch a special explanatory
HELP box:

**Press Esc
at any time
to close
down a
HELP window or
box.**

data type

The attribute of a variable or field that
determines what kind of data it can hold.
For example, the Text and Memo field data
types allow the field to store either text or
numbers, but the Number data type will
allow only numbers to be stored in the field.
Number data type fields store numerical
data that will be used in mathematical
calculations. Use the Currency data type to
display or calculate currency values.
Supported data types include field data
types, Visual Basic data types, and query
parameter data types.

Using the Access HELP system (3)

REMEMBER **Access calls these highly specific HELP bubbles 'ToolTips'. ToolTips are a specialised form of ScreenTips (see below).**

Other HELP features Access supports include the following:

- moving the mouse pointer over toolbar buttons produces an explanatory HELP bubble:

REMEMBER **Access calls these highly specific HELP topics 'ScreenTips'.**

- moving the mouse pointer over fields in dialogs, commands or screen areas and right-clicking produces a specific HELP box. Carry out the following procedure to activate this.

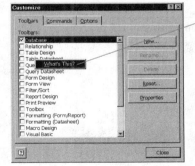

Left-click here for the specific help topic

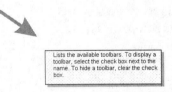

REMEMBER **The Office Assistant is only available to Access 97 users. If you're using Access 95, however, you can use an earlier version: the Answer Wizard. See pages 18-20.**

Other standard Windows 95 HELP features are also present; see your Windows documentation for how to use these.

Access also has one additional HELP feature: the Office Assistant. The Office Assistant is unique to Microsoft Office applications.

The Office Assistant (1)

Access 97 has a unique HELP feature, designed to make it much easier to become productive: the Office Assistant. The Office Assistant:

To hide the Office Assistant, right-click it. In the menu, click Hide Assistant.

- answers questions directly. This is an especially useful feature for the reason that, normally when you invoke a program's HELP system, you know more or less the question you want to ask, or the topic on which you need information. If neither of these is true, however, the Office Assistant responds to plain English questions and provides a choice of answers. For example, responses produced by entering 'What are ToolTips?' include:

  — Show or hide shortcut keys in ToolTips

  — Show or hide toolbar ScreenTips

  — Turn ScreenTips off

The Office Assistant is animated. It can also change shape! To do this, click the Options button: In the dialog which appears, activate the Gallery tab. Click the Next button until the Assistant you want is displayed. Then click OK.

- provides context-sensitive tips

- offers HELP which relates specifically to Access 97

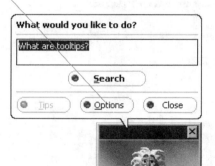

The Office Assistant, after it has just launched

If the Assistant HELP bubble isn't displayed, simply click anywhere in the Assistant.

The Office Assistant (2) New in Access 97

 If the Office Assistant isn't on-screen when a tip is launched, the toolbar button which launches it changes to:

 The bulb denotes a latent tip

Launching the Office Assistant

By default, the Office Assistant displays automatically. If it isn't currently on-screen, however, refer to the Database toolbar and do the following:

Click here

Displaying tips

Ensure the Office Assistant is on-screen. Then do the following:

 **Sometimes, the Office Assistant itself will indicate that it has a tip which may be useful:**

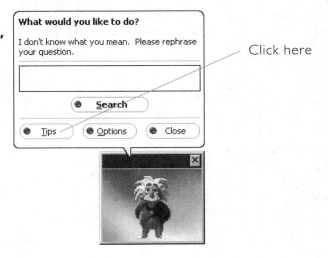

Click here

Click here to view a suggested tip

A context-sensitive tip appears. Do the following when you've finished with it:

Click here

 Click Next or Back (if available) to view another tip:

The Office Assistant New in Access 97

Users of Access 95 can't use the Office Assistant. However, they can use the Answer Wizard to get help with specific questions.

Pull down the Help menu and click Answer Wizard. In the uppermost field in the Answer Wizard, type in your question. Click Search. In the lower (and larger) field, double-click the relevant topic.

Previous versions of Access had a feature called the Answer Wizard. This allowed you to enter questions in plain English. The advantage of using the Answer Wizard was that you could use it to find information on topics which you weren't sure how to classify.

The Office Assistant incorporates an improved version of the Answer Wizard.

Asking questions

First, ensure the Office Assistant is visible. Then do the following:

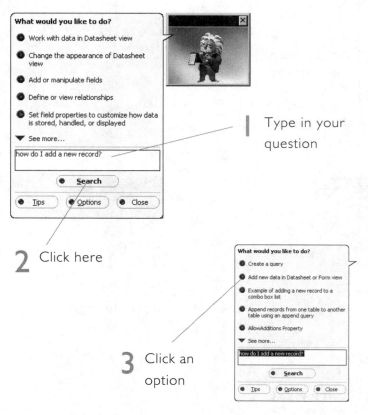

Type in your question

2 Click here

3 Click an option

To close an Office Assistant or Answer Wizard window at any time, press Esc.

Re step 3 – if none of the topics are suitable, click See More (if available). Then click the correct option in the new list.

Your first database

Chapter Two

This chapter shows you how to create new databases. First, we'll discuss elements you need to sort out *before* you start. Then you'll learn how to create a simple database manually, and also how to create more complex examples by automating the process with Database Wizards. You'll also discover how to open databases you've already created, including (for Access 97 users) those stored on the World Wide Web. Finally, you'll save your work to disk (and to the World Wide Web).

Covers

Database terminology (1)

Before you can learn to use Access to create databases, you need to be familiar with and understand the following terms:

Database   Information grouped together (and organised for ease of reference) into an Access file

Tables   Used to store data in rows and columns, like a spreadsheet

Records   (Horizontal) rows of data in tables. Each record is a complete set of related data items (for instance, in a magazine's subscription database each record is the information associated with each subscriber)

Fields   (Vertical) columns of data in tables. Fields are spaces reserved for specified data (for instance, subscription payment details for all records in a magazine database might be kept in a field called 'Renewals')

REMEMBER

This is an extract from a table associated with the Membership Wizard. It's filled with sample data, for illustration purposes.

Fields

First Name	Last Name	Home Address	City
Karl	Jablonski	722 DaVinci Blv	Kirkland
Elizabeth	Lincoln	1900 Oak St.	Vancouver
Nancy	Davolio	507 - 20th Ave.	Seattle
Janet	Leverling	4110 Old Redm	Redmond
Laura	Callahan	4726 - 11th Ave	Seattle
Steven	Buchanan	Coventry House	London
Hari	Kumar	90 Wadhurst R	London
Patricio	Simpson	Cerrito 333	Buenos Aires
Yoshi	Latimer	2732 Baker Blv	Eugene
Lino	Rodriguez	Estrada da saú	Lisboa
Art	Braunschweiger		
Robert	King	7 Houndstooth F	London
*			

Records

Database terminology (2)

Query	The process by which data can be extracted from tables in accordance with criteria you specify. Queries represent ways of viewing fields from more than one table or query in the same record

REMEMBER

This is an extract from a form associated with the Membership Wizard. It's filled with sample data, for illustration purposes.

Forms	You use forms to display table or query data in a customised format. As with queries, forms can host information from one or more tables or queries

Fields

REMEMBER

Forms display one record at a time, and are often the most convenient way to interact with your data.

Member ID	2	Home Phone	(609) 555-3392
First Name	Elizabeth	Member Type	Full Member
Last Name	Lincoln	Date Joined	30/05/92
Home Address	1900 Oak St.	Send Inv. To Work	
City	Vancouver	Member Dues	£45.00
State/Province	B.C.	Amount Paid	£45.00
Postal Code	V3F 2K1	Amount Due	£0.00
Country	Canada		

Committees... Payments... Preview Invoice... Dial... Page: 1 2

Record: 2 of 12

Fields

REMEMBER

Tables, queries, forms and reports are all 'objects'. In Access, objects are items which can be selected and manipulated.

Reports	Use reports to display table or query data in a customised format (with page numbers and headings). Reports can't be edited, but they can contain data from one or more tables or queries

The pre-planning stage

Before you start to create a database, it's a good idea to plan it out first. This can save you a lot of time and effort. Consider implementing the following suggestions:

- If you'll be basing your new database on an existing one (manual or computerised), study the ways in which your data is currently organised. This will help when it comes to creating Access tables and queries.

- Make sure you're clear in your own mind about the categories into which data can be split logically. For example, a magazine would clearly wish to have a section where subscription details were maintained, and arguably a separate section for payment details.

- Plan out which fields you want your new database to have. For example, a magazine (and most other database types) would need fields relating to:

  — Client names

  — Addresses

  — Phone numbers

A table excerpt from a database created with the Membership Wizard; logically, this field could be the primary key:

- Determine which fields within specific tables can serve as 'primary keys'. The primary key is the field which is common to each record, and which identifies it as being unique. In our magazine example, this could well be the Member ID field. Primary keys are also used by Access to determine the order in which records are sorted, and to speed up query processing.

Member ID	First Name	Last Name	Home Address
1	Karl	Jablonski	722 DaVinci Blv
2	Elizabeth	Lincoln	1900 Oak St.
3	Nancy	Davolio	507 - 20th Ave.
4	Janet	Leverling	4110 Old Redm
5	Laura	Callahan	4726 - 11th Ave
6	Steven	Buchanan	Coventry House
7	Hari	Kumar	90 Wadhurst Rd
8	Patricio	Simpson	Cerrito 333
9	Yoshi	Latimer	2732 Baker Blv
10	Lino	Rodriguez	Estrada da saú
11	Art	Braunschweiger	
12	Robert	King	7 Houndstooth F
(AutoNumber)			

Creating databases – an overview

There are two ways to create new databases in Access:

- using an appropriate wizard

- manually

Both approaches have their merits. The manual method provides more precision: you create a blank database and then include the necessary components over a period of time. This method gives you complete control over the make-up of your database, but the process can easily become long-winded. The various 'Starting Access' topics in Chapter 1 show you how to use this technique to create a very simple database *at the same time as you start Access*. (Or see the 'Creating databases manually' topics later for how to do this when Access is already running.)

HANDY TIP

See the techniques discussed in later chapters for how to customise and supplement manually created databases.

The wizard method, on the other hand, is much easier to use, far more convenient and just as effective. You can select and apply the Database Wizard you need (there are 22 to choose from). When you do so, the wizard automatically inserts the necessary objects in accordance with your specifications.

Database Wizards let you specify:

- the overall form background (you can choose from 10 preset colours and patterns)

- report styles

- which tables and fields should be included

- an overall database title

Although they don't permit the same complexity as the manual method, wizards do have the advantage of creating databases which are tailor-made for the purpose for which they were designed. They represent a fast, convenient and detailed method for the creation of databases.

Whichever method you use to create a database, you can easily amend it later.

Creating databases manually (1)

For how to create a database manually *just after you've launched Access, see the 'Starting Access' topics in Section 1.*

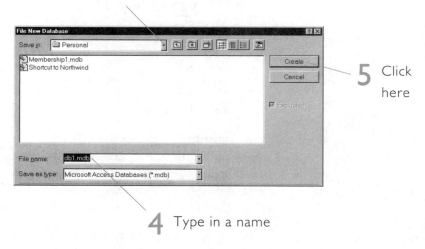

HANDY TIP

To create a database manually from within Access, pull down the File menu and click New Database. Now do the following:

Activate this tab

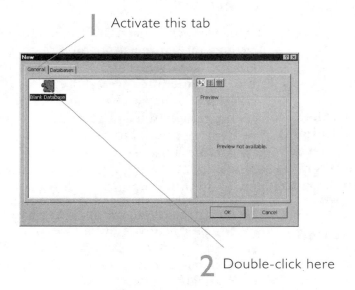

2 Double-click here

3 Click here; select the drive/folder you
want to host the new database

5 Click
here

4 Type in a name

Creating databases manually (2)

There are two further dialogs which have to be negotiated. After step 3 below, Access creates a database table. (But see the Handy Tip for help with automating the entire process of table creation.)

Click here

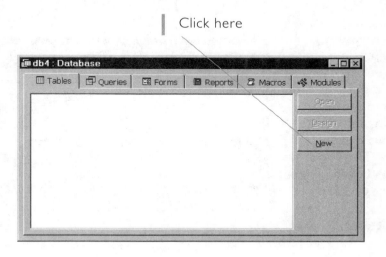

HANDY TIP

Re step 2 – at this point you can, if you want to, automate the creation of a table with the use of a wizard. See the 'Automating table creation' topics in Chapter 3 for how to do this.

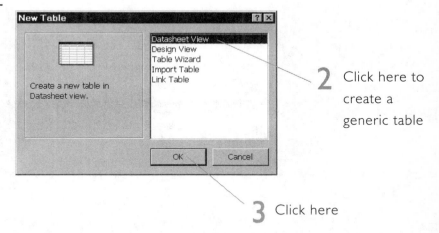

2 Click here to create a generic table

3 Click here

Automating database creation (1)

To create a database with the help of the Database Wizard, pull down the File menu and click New Database. Now do the following:

Database Wizards consist of several stages, each represented by a specific dialog. The precise content varies somewhat from wizard to wizard. The Address Book Wizard produces a less complex database than others.

Ensure the Databases tab is active

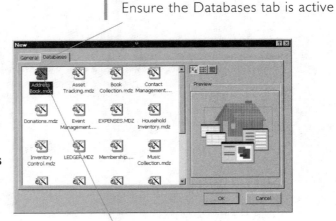

2 Double-click the appropriate database type

3 Click here; select the drive/folder you want to host the new database

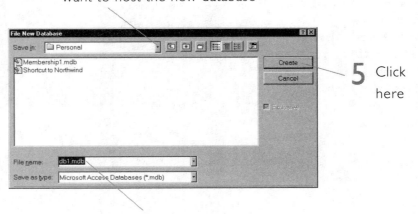

5 Click here

4 Type in a name

Automating database creation (2)

Do the following:

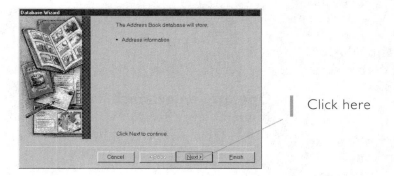

| Click here

Access now launches additional dialogs relating to the following aspects of database creation:

- specifying which fields each table contains

- allocating an overall look (screen display style)

- allocating a report style

- allocating a database title

Complete the dialogs as appropriate, then carry out the following steps:

2 Optional – ensure this is selected to have Access open the new database automatically

REMEMBER

After step 3, Access creates the new database. The process can sometimes take a little while...

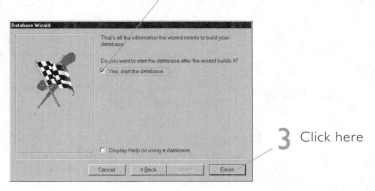

3 Click here

Opening existing databases (1)

 You can also open databases directly from the World Wide Web – see page 32.

 You can use a further method to open recently used databases: the Documents section of the Windows Start menu. (See your Windows documentation for how to do this.)

We've just seen how Access lets you create new databases in various ways. Once you've done this, you'll need to open them for editing. You can open existing databases:

- in the process of starting Access

- from within Access

Opening a database at startup

Immediately after you've started Access, carry out steps 1 and 2, OR 1 and 3, as appropriate:

Click here

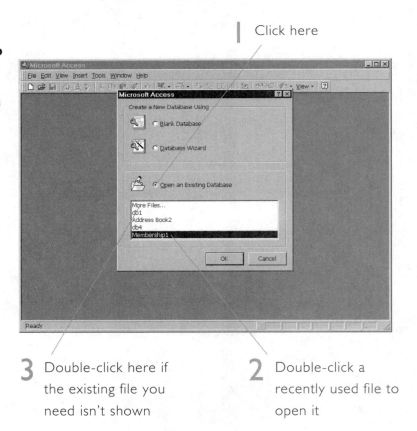

3 Double-click here if the existing file you need isn't shown

2 Double-click a recently used file to open it

If you follow steps 1 and 3, the Open dialog appears. See page 31 for how to complete this.

Opening existing databases (2)

Opening a database from within Access

Pull down the File menu and click Open. Now carry out the following steps, as appropriate:

You can use a keyboard shortcut to launch the Open dialog: simply press Ctrl+O.

2 Click here. In the drop-down list, click the drive/folder which hosts the file

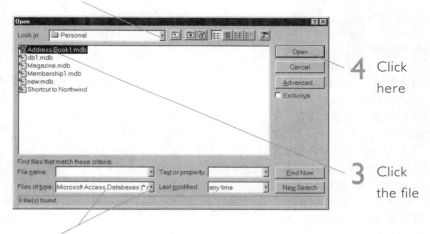

4 Click here

3 Click the file

| Make sure *Microsoft Access Databases* is shown. If it isn't, click the arrow and select it from the drop-down list

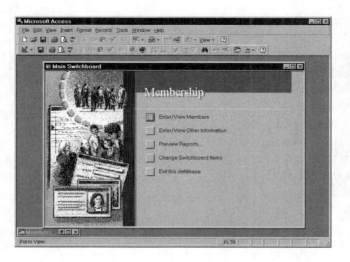

The opened database

Opening Web databases New in Access 97

REMEMBER

To open Web databases, you must have access to the Internet (e.g. via a service provider), and you must have installed a modem. Additionally, your connection must be open when you carry out the procedures listed here.

(For advice on the Internet in general, read a companion volume: 'Internet UK in easy steps'.)

You can open databases stored at any HTTP site on the World Wide Web.

If the Web toolbar isn't currently on-screen, move the mouse pointer over any existing toolbar and right-click. In the menu which appears, click Web. Now do the following:

Click here

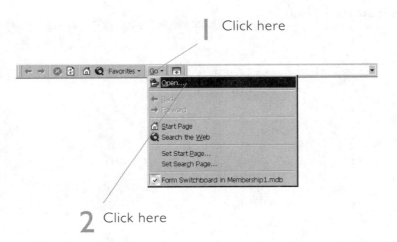

2 Click here

HANDY TIP

If you don't know the site address, don't follow step 3. Instead, click the Browse button. Use the Browse dialog (a variant of the Open dialog discussed on page 31) to locate it. Click Open. Then follow step 4 on page 31.

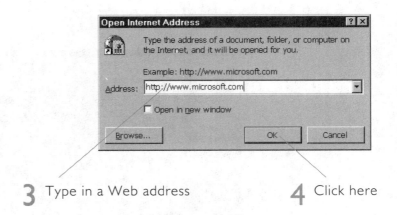

3 Type in a Web address

4 Click here

Save operations

Most programs require you to save your work at frequent intervals, in order to avoid data loss in the event of a hardware fault or power interruption. However, Access does this for you. Access automatically saves the record you're working on whenever you:

- move the insertion point to a different record

- close the active form or datasheet

- close the relevant database

- close down Access itself

You can also save your work manually, if you want (for instance, if you suspect that Windows is about to crash). You can save the active record, or the complete database (including the various layout and design components).

Saving the active record
Pull down the Records menu and do the following:

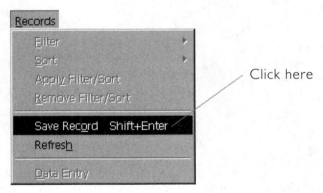

Click here

Saving databases
To save the whole database, pull down the File menu and click Save.

Saving to the Web New in Access 97

Re step 2 – to publish your databases on the Web, you must have access to the Internet (e.g. via a service provider), and you must have installed a modem. For help with step 2, consult your service provider. For more information on the Internet in general, read a companion volume: 'Internet UK in easy steps'.

Access 97 users can save Access databases to any HTTP site on the World Wide Web. This is a two-stage process:

1. saving your completed database in HTML (HyperText Markup Language) format

2. copying the HTML files to your service provider

Step 2 is outside the scope of this book.

Pull down the File menu and click Save as HTML. Access now launches the Publish to the Web Wizard. This consists of six dialogs. The first is shown below. Do the following:

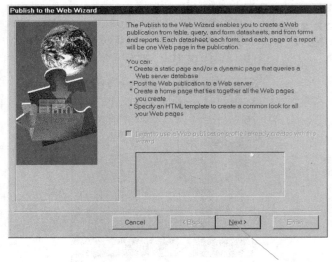

Click here

In later dialogs, you do the following:

- **select components**
- **apply a template**
- **pick an HTML format**
- **specify where the HTML file is saved**
- **specify if you want a 'home page' created**
- **specify if you want your formatting saved as a 'profile' for future use**

Now complete the additional Wizard dialogs which appear (in each case, click the Next button to continue). Finally, do the following in the last dialog:

 Click here

Creating tables

This chapter shows you how to create new tables. First, you'll learn how to automate the process with a wizard. Then you'll discover how to create a simple table manually. You'll also import tables in third-party formats (including – if you're using Access 97 – HTML tables on the World Wide Web). You'll create your own fields, allocate data types to them and customise field properties. Finally, you'll save your work and export it in third-party formats.

Chaper Three

Covers

Tables – an overview

After you've created an Access database, the next step is to create the tables which store your data. This is essential if you created the database manually. If, on the other hand, you used a Database Wizard to create your database, you'll already have one or more tailor-made tables ready to use – even then, however, you'll probably want to create your own at some time. The procedures outlined in this chapter apply to both scenarios.

There are two basic ways to create a table:

•   manually

•   with the help of the Table Wizard

Both approaches have their merits. On the one hand, the manual method provides more precision: you create a blank table and then (in a separate operation) include whatever fields you wish. You can also customise the field formats. This method gives you complete control over the make-up of your table, but the overall process is relatively time-consuming.

The wizard method, on the other hand, is much easier to use, and far more convenient. You can:

•   choose from a selection of table types

•   choose from a selection of table designs

•   enter data into the table

•   enter data into a form created by the Wizard

Although using the Table Wizard doesn't permit the same complexity as the manual method, it does represent a fast, convenient, detailed and effective method for the creation of tables.

Whichever method you use to create a table, you can easily amend it later.

The Database window

The Database window may appear as a minimised bar in the bottom left-hand corner of the screen:

Click here to restore (expand) it.

Access 97 users can import tables from the World Wide Web if they have:
- **live access to the Internet**
- **an installed modem.**

Follow the procedures in the Handy Tip on page 36 but select:

HTML Documents (*html;*.htm)

in the 'Files of type' field. Double-click the relevant HTML file name. Finally, complete the Import HTML Wizard, as appropriate.

When you create a new database in Access (or open an existing one), the Database window displays. Since this is the basis for table creation, we need to discuss this before we move on.

The illustration below shows a small, manually created database:

Magnified view of Close button

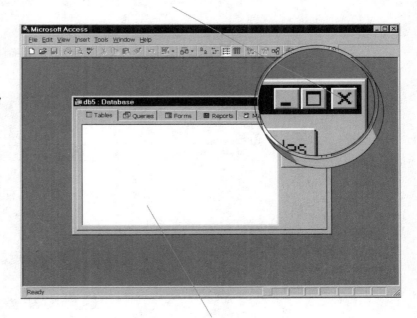

Database window

The Database window can be thought of as a command centre for the active database. For example, clicking on the Close button closes the database. It's also the basis from which much of the work you carry out with tables, queries, forms and reports is undertaken.

Automating table creation (1)

To create a table with the help of the Table Wizard, first make sure that the Database window is visible (see the 'Database window' topic earlier for how to do this). Then do the following:

Activate the Tables tab

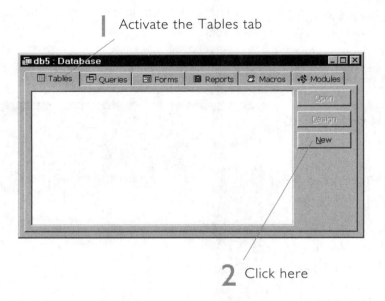

2 Click here

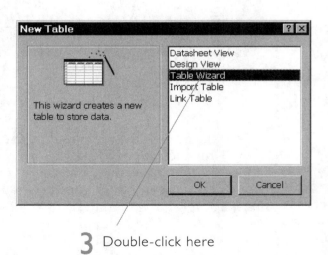

3 Double-click here

Automating table creation (2)

Access now launches the Table Wizard. Do the following:

2 Select a sample table

3 Double-click the field(s) you want to include

If you want to rename fields, click the Rename Field button just after you've carried out step 3.

Type in a new name, then click OK. Now carry out step 4.

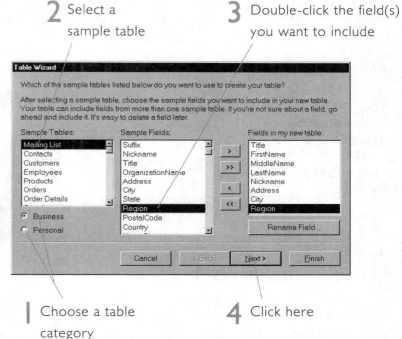

| Choose a table category

4 Click here

5 Type in a name for your table

Re step 6 – it's usually preferable (and quicker) to let Access select a primary key for you. You can always allocate a new key later, if you want.

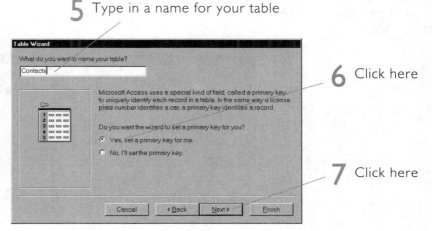

6 Click here

7 Click here

Automating table creation (3)

The next stage in the process of table creation has to do with relationships. Often when you build a new table, one or more of the records will be held in common with other tables. When this is so, you need to tell Access what the precise relationship is.

REMEMBER

If your new table has no common records, simply omit steps 1-3 inclusive. Instead, merely follow step 4.

REMEMBER

If this is the first table you've created in the current database, neither of the dialogs shown here display. Instead, proceed directly to page 41.

Do the following:

1. Click here if your new table is related to another

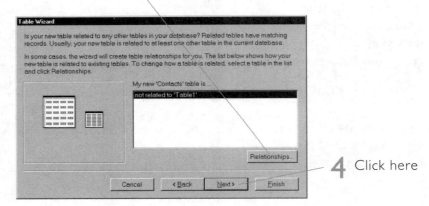

4 Click here

2. Click the appropriate relationship option

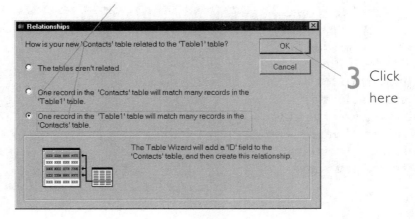

3 Click here

Automating table creation (4)

The Table Wizard is now almost ready to create your table. When it has done so, you'll probably want to begin entering data more or less immediately. Access lets you do this in two ways:

- directly into the table

- into a form built by the wizard

Each of these techniques has its own particular merits; you can specify which you prefer now.

The table method is more suitable for the rapid entering of information in bulk, while the form method is more visually appealing and – arguably – makes your data easier to work with.

Carry out the following steps:

HANDY TIP **You can also opt to have Access let you customise the design of your table when the wizard has completed it. See the 'Amending table design' topics (and others) later for how to do this.**

Click a data entry option

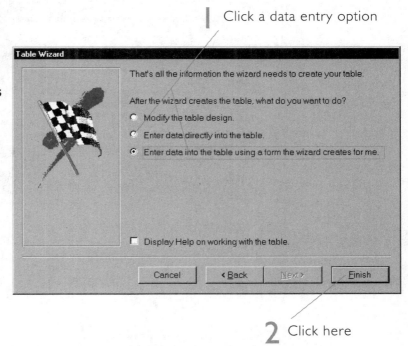

Click here

Automating table creation (5)

The Table Wizard now launches one of the following (according to which option you chose in step 1 on page 41):

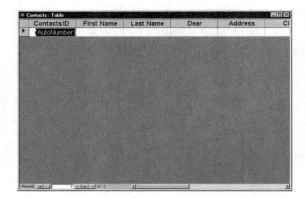

A table containing a single blank record

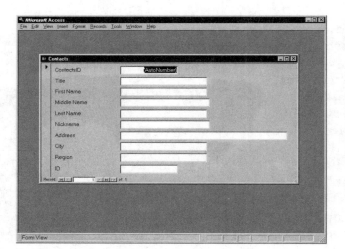

A form showing the first (blank) record in the new table

You can now begin entering data into your new table. (For how to do this, see Chapter 5).

Creating tables manually

To create a table from scratch, first make sure that the Database window is visible (see 'The Database window' earlier for how to do this). Then carry out the following steps:

| Activate the Tables tab

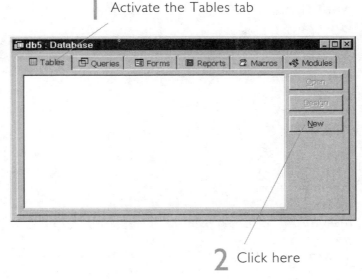

2 Click here

After step 3, Access creates the new table:

Refer to the 'Amending table design' topics later for how to customise it.

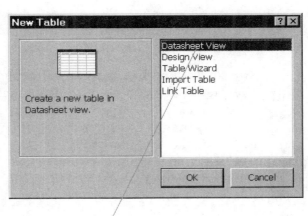

3 Double-click here

Table design – an overview

Now that you've created a table manually, you need to customise the field conformation. This involves specifying the following information:

If you want to, you can also opt to redesign tables created with the Table Wizard.

- names

- data types

- format/field size

- additional field properties

You can choose from several data types. The main ones are:

Text	Use for text and numbers which don't require calculations performed on them (e.g. phone numbers)
Memo	Use for annotations (text and numbers)
Number	Use for calculable numbers
Date/Time	Use for dates (within the year range 100 to 9,999) and times
Currency	Self-explanatory
AutoNumber	Access uses this to identify records automatically and sequentially

Access 97 users can also apply an additional data type:
Hyperlink
The only field property you'll normally need to set for this data type is 'Caption'. For example, if you insert a hyperlinked field containing Internet addresses into a table, you might apply this caption to it:
Home Page
See Chapter 5 for more information on using hyperlinks.

The field properties you can set depend on the data type allocated. For example, in fields which have had *Text* allocated as a data type you can specify (among other features) the maximum number of characters data entries can have. On the other hand, if *Date/Time* is the data type, you can choose from a variety of date and time formats (e.g. '12 May 1998' or '12/05/98').

Another example: if you allocate *Number* as the data type, you can set the number of decimal places Access uses to display numbers in the relevant field, and you can determine whether scientific notation is used (e.g. 2.16E +03).

Amending table design (1)

There are two ways to begin customising a table's design.

If the table is already open
Pull down the View menu and do the following:

Access 95 users should follow a slightly different procedure here.
Pull down the View menu and click Table Design.

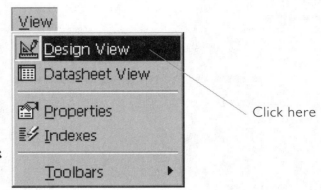

Click here

If the table isn't already open
Go to the Database window (see page 37 for how to do this) and carry out the following steps:

Activate the Tables tab

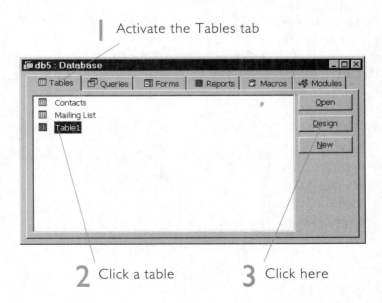

2 Click a table

3 Click here

Amending table design (2)

REMEMBER

In Access 95, the Design View window was known as the Table Design window.

The Design View window now launches. This is the basis for adding and customising fields. There are two sections:

- the Field Format pane

- the Field Properties pane

Field Format pane

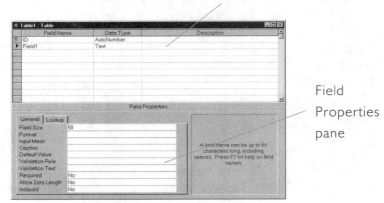

Field Properties pane

REMEMBER

In this instance, the first field in the table (its function is to enter a unique ID reference automatically) was inserted by Access and needs no reformatting.

Applying a name and data type

Before you can specify field characteristics, you need to name the new field and apply a data type.

Do the following:

Type in a name

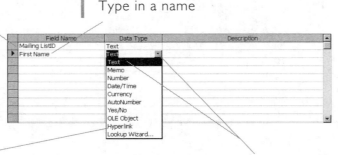

REMEMBER

Re step 2 – the Hyperlink option is only available to Access 97 users.
  See Chapter 5 for how to insert/work with hyperlinks.

2 Click here; select a data type in the list

Setting Text properties (1)

The next few topics explore the main customisation options which result from specific data types.

When a field has the Text data type associated with it, you may need to specify:

The character limit

The character maximum for Text fields is 255; often, fields will benefit from having far fewer (one advantage is that Access processes them more quickly).

A caption

'Captions' in Access are special titles which only display in forms.

A default value

Default values are text and/or numerals which you want to appear in every instance of the field (e.g. you might wish the Country field in a Contacts database to show 'U.K.' permanently).

Indexing

Implementing indexing in a database often (but not always) enables Access to find and sort records faster (if it knows where information is, it can usually reach it more rapidly). Indexing only applies to the Text, Number, Currency and Date/Time data types. Fields which have had a primary key allocated are automatically indexed. When you index a field, you can specify whether duplicated values are allowed; for instance, you may want to allow duplicate names in a 'Surname' field.

You should index fields you use frequently, and which contain a wide variety of data. An obvious choice for most databases would be the field which contains surname details.

Setting Text properties (2)

In Access 95, the Design View window was known as the Table Design window.

Launch the Design View window (see the 'Amending Table design (1) topic for how to do this). Then carry out any of steps 1-4 below. If you carry out step 4, also follow step 5 OR 6:

The arrow indicates that a field has been selected and is being redesigned.

Re step 4 – to make the ☑ appear, first click in the relevant field to the left.

1 Type in a character limit

2 Type in a caption

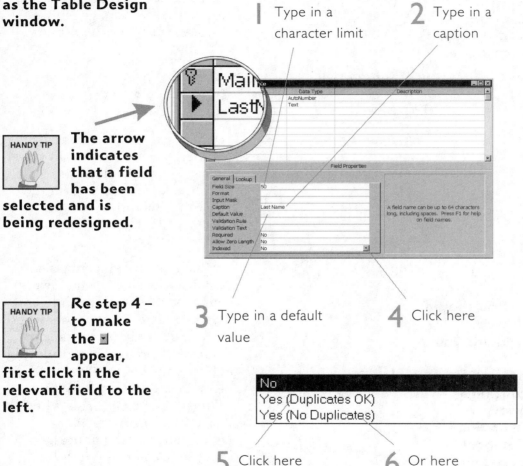

3 Type in a default value

4 Click here

5 Click here

6 Or here

Setting Number properties (1)

If you set a field's data type to Number, features you can specify include:

Field Size

You can choose from a variety of settings. The main ones are:

Integer – stores *whole* numbers in the range -32,768 to 32,767

Long Integer – stores *whole* numbers in the range -2,147,483,648 to +2,147,483,647

Single – stores positive numbers in the range: 1.401298E-45 to +3.402823E38

 You can also set properties that have already been discussed. For example, you can index fields which have had the Number data type applied.

Format

You can specify the number format for a field's contents. The main choices are:

General Number – numbers display as entered

Fixed – numbers display with two decimal places

Standard – as Fixed, but Access denotes thousands with a comma (e.g. 3,267.12)

Percent – Access multiplies inserted values by 100 and adds '%'

Decimal Places

You can specify how many places numerical values should be expressed to.

The acceptable range is 0 to 15.

Setting Number properties (2)

In Access 95, the Design View window was known as the Table Design window.

Launch the Design View window (see the 'Amending table design (1)' topic for how to do this). Then carry out any of steps 1-3 below. If you carry out step 1, also follow step 4. Steps 2 and 3 should be followed by 5 and 6 respectively:

Click here

Re steps 1, 2 and 3 – to make the ▾ **appear,** first click in the relevant field to the left.

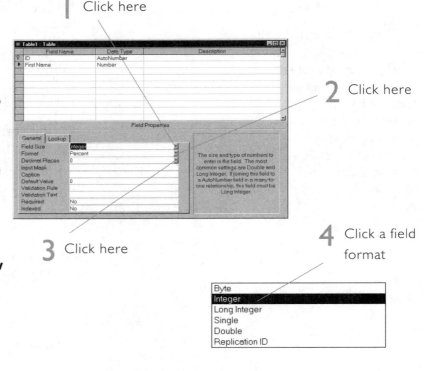

2 Click here

3 Click here

4 Click a field format

Steps 4, 5 and 6 show subsidiary windows which launch according to whether you follow steps 1, 2 or 3 respectively.

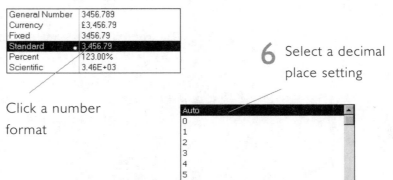

5 Click a number format

6 Select a decimal place setting

Re step 6 – select Auto if you want the choice you made in steps 1 and 4 to determine the number of decimal places.

Setting Date/Time properties (1)

If you set a field's data type to Date/Time, there are fewer available features (and many of them have already been discussed in earlier topics). However, you do need to be familiar with the following:

Format

You can specify the date and/or time formats for a field's contents. The choices are:

General Date – displays dates and/or times as Windows 95 itself does (e.g. 05/06/98 09:00:12 PM)

Short Date – same as the date component of the General Date option (e.g. 6-8-98)

Medium Date – a halfway house (e.g. 1-Apr-98)

Long Date – shows dates in full (e.g. Tuesday, May 19, 1998)

Short Time – shows times as an irreducible minimum (e.g. 13.45)

Medium Time – displays slightly more information than the Short Time option, and doesn't use the 24-hour clock (e.g. 08:32 PM)

Long Time – same as the time component of the General Date option (e.g. 11:52:36 PM)

Setting Date/Time properties (2)

In Access 95, the Design View window was known as the Table Design window.

Launch the Design View window (see the 'Amending table design (1)' topic for how to do this). Then carry out steps 1 and 2 below:

Re step 1 – to make the ⏷ appear, first click in the relevant field to the left.

Click here

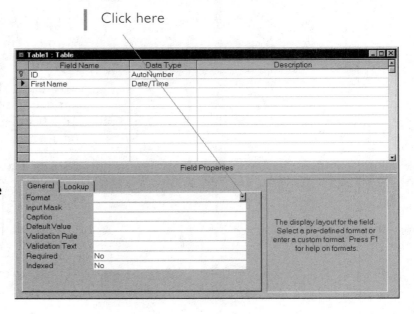

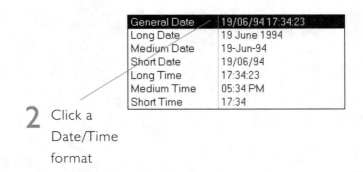

2 Click a Date/Time format

Setting Currency properties

When you allocate Currency as a field's data type, many of the options are more or less identical with those associated with Number. For instance, you can allocate the same Format and Decimal Place options.

Launch the Table Design window (see the 'Amending table design (1) topic for how to do this). Then carry out steps 1 and/or 2 below, followed by 3 and 4 respectively:

Re steps 1 and 2 – to make the ▾ appear, first click in the relevant field to the left.

Click here

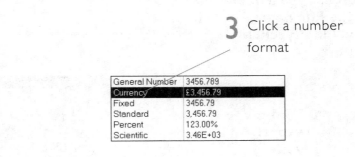

2 Click here

Steps 3 and 4 show subsidiary windows which launch according to whether you follow step 1 or 2 respectively.

3 Click a number format

Re step 4 – select Auto if you want the choice you made in steps 1 and 3 to determine the number of decimal places.

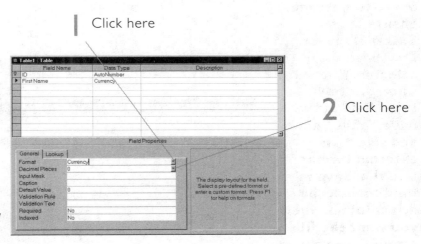

4 Select a decimal place setting

Saving your design work

You can also export your work to third-party formats.

Pull down the File menu and click Save As/Export. In the Save As message, ensure 'To an External File or Database' is selected. Click OK. Click the 'Save as type' field in the Save Table... dialog and select an external format. Use the 'Save in' field to pick the drive/folder where you want the file stored. Type a name in the File name box. Finally, click Export.

When you've finished designing table fields, it's necessary to save your work to disk. This is a two-stage process and involves:

• closing the Table Design window

• responding appropriately to a warning message

Do the following:

Click here

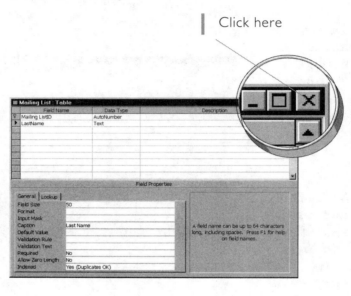

For how to export your databases onto the World Wide Web, see page 34.

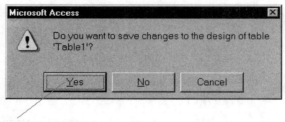

2 Click here

Creating forms

This chapter shows you how to create new forms. First, you'll learn how to automate the process with AutoForm and the Form Wizard. Then you'll discover how to create a simple form manually. You'll apply preset format schemes to it; add fields and labels; import forms from other databases; and customise field/label formats individually. Access 97 users will also create tabbed controls and then apply the relevant fields/labels. Finally, you'll save your work to disk.

Covers

Chapter Four

Forms – an overview

AutoForm is a kind of 'mini-wizard'; it produces simplified forms automatically, based on existing database tables.

You can import forms from other Access databases. In the Database window, pull down the File menu and click Get External Data, Import. Click the 'Files of type' field in the Import dialog and select *Microsoft Access*. Use the 'Look in' field to select the drive/folder for the file which hosts the form you want to import. Double-click the file name. In the Import Objects dialog, click the Forms tab. Double-click the form you want to import.

Once you've created an Access database and (possibly one or more tables to go with it), you may well wish to create forms to view your data in a more 'user-friendly' way. If you used a Database Wizard to create your database, you'll already have one or more tailor-made forms ready to use (even then, however, you may well want to create your own at some time). If, on the other hand, you created the database manually, you'll have to create any forms you need. The procedures outlined in this chapter apply to both scenarios.

There are three ways to create a form:

- using AutoForm

- with the help of the Form Wizard

- manually

All three approaches have their merits. On the one hand, the manual method provides more precision: you create a blank form and then (in a separate operation) include whatever fields you wish. You can also customise the field formats. This method gives you complete control over the make-up of your form, but the overall process is relatively time-consuming.

The wizard/AutoForm methods, on the other hand, are far easier to use. For instance, the Form Wizard lets you:

- choose from three form layouts

- choose from a selection of form styles

- specify which tables/fields are included

Although using AutoForm or the Form Wizard doesn't permit the same complexity as the manual method, it does represent a fast, convenient, detailed and effective method for the creation of forms.

Whichever method you use to create a form, you can easily amend it later.

Using AutoForm

To create a form with Access' AutoForm feature, first make sure that the Database window is visible (see page 37 in Chapter 3 for how to do this). Then do the following:

In forms created with AutoForm, all fields and records in the base table display. Each field appears on a separate line.

Activate the Tables tab

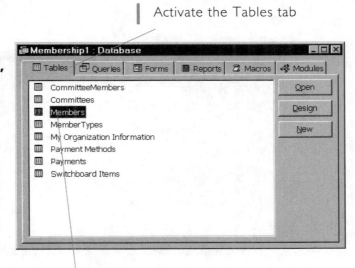

2 Double-click the table on which you want to base the form

This is the Table Datasheet toolbar. (The Access 95 equivalent is the Database toolbar.) Most toolbars contain the ⊞ (New Object) button.

3 Click here

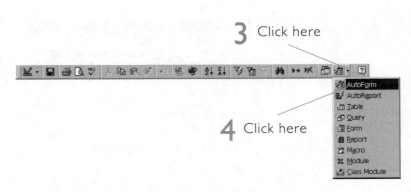

4 Click here

Automating form creation (1)

To create a form with the help of the Form Wizard, first make sure that the Database window is visible (see page 37 in Chapter 3 for how to do this). Then do the following:

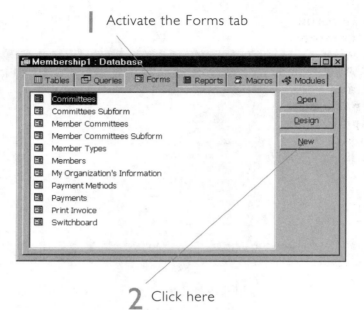

1 Activate the Forms tab

2 Click here

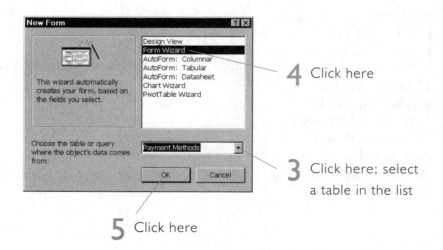

4 Click here

3 Click here; select a table in the list

5 Click here

Automating form creation (2)

Re step 1 – in step 3 on page 58, you selected a table on which to base the new form. If you want to use fields from *additional* tables, click here: Select a new table from the list. Finally, carry out steps 2-4.

Access now launches the Form Wizard. Carry out the following steps:

Double-click the field(s) you want to include

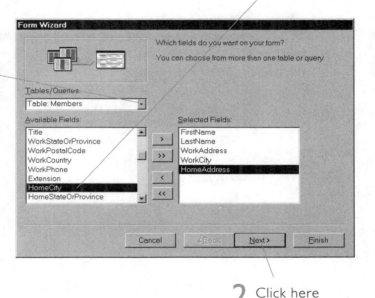

2 Click here

Re step 3 – the 'Justified' option is only available to Access 97 users.

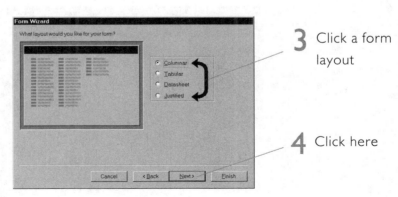

3 Click a form layout

4 Click here

Automating form creation (3)

In the final stage of the process of form creation, you select the overall style you want your new form to have. This is especially important in the case of forms because they're highly visual. Do the following:

Click a style

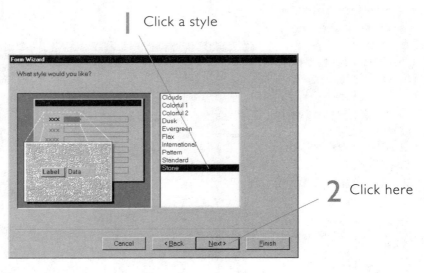

2 Click here

3 Name the new form

4 Click here to have Access open the new form after step 5

5 Click here

Automating form creation (4)

The Form Wizard now creates your new form. It then opens it for editing.

The illustrations below show two varieties of form (according to whether you selected Columnar or Tabular as the basic layout in step 3 on page 59):

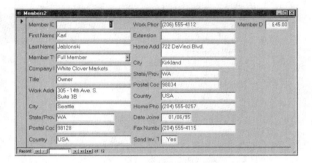

The
Columnar
form

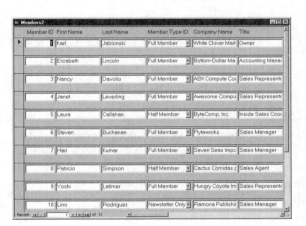

The
Tabular
form

Whichever form layout you selected, you can now begin entering data into your new form.

For how to do this, see Chapter 5.

Creating forms manually

To create a form from scratch, first make sure that the Database window is visible (see page 37 in Chapter 3 for how to do this). Then carry out the following steps:

Activate the Forms tab

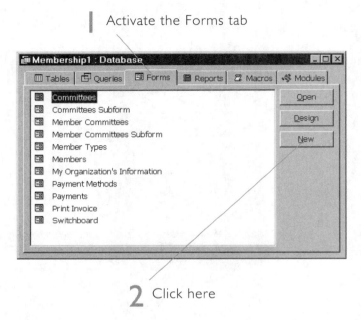

2 Click here

After step 5, Access creates the new form. See the 'Amending form design' topics later (and others) for how to customise it.

REMEMBER

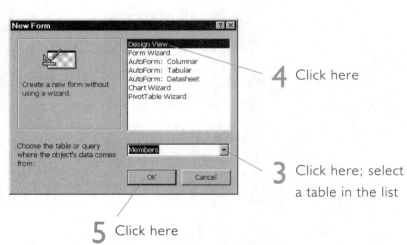

4 Click here

3 Click here; select a table in the list

5 Click here

Form design – an overview

HANDY TIP

If you want to, you can also opt to redesign forms created with the Form Wizard.

HANDY TIP

To see what your work looks like, now or at any stage in the form design process, pull down the View menu and click Form View. To continue your design work, pull down the same menu and click Design View.
N.B. Access 95 users should use a slightly different procedure. Click Form in the View menu to view the underlying form, and Form Design to restart design work.

Now that you've created a form manually, you must add the various fields and labels (explanatory classifications) you need. Access calls everything you add to a form a 'control'. There are two main types:

*   bound

*   unbound

Bound controls pull in data from fields in an underlying database table. For instance, if a field in a table contains post code information, the relevant control will return post code data for the currently active record.

Unbound controls, on the other hand, contain supplementary text (e.g. instructions to the database user) or graphics components (e.g. lines); they aren't connected to table fields.

The distinction is made clear in the following:

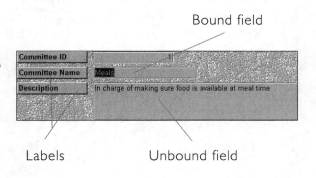

Bound field

Bound and unbound fields in a form extract

Labels   Unbound field

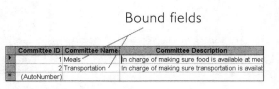

Bound fields

Bound fields in the original table

Customising form design is much more visual than customising tables.

Amending form design (1)

There are two ways to begin customising a form's design.

If the form is already open
Pull down the View menu and do the following:

 Here, Access 95 users should pull down the View menu and click Form Design.

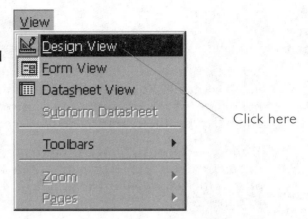

Click here

If the form isn't already open
Go to the Database window (see page 37 in Chapter 3 for how to do this) and do the following:

Activate the Forms tab

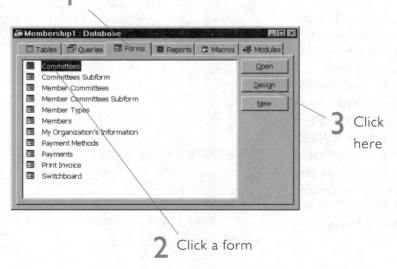

3 Click here

2 Click a form

Amending form design (2)

If the Field List isn't currently visible, pull down the View menu and click Field List.

Access now launches the form in Design View. This is the basis for adding and customising fields. The following components are especially important:

- the Detail pane
- the Toolbox
- the Field List

Here, the Detail pane is uncluttered
because this is a manually created form. Detail panes for forms created with the Form Wizard or AutoForm will be more complex.

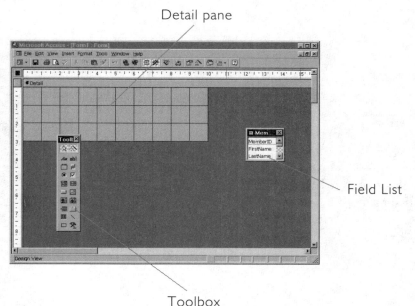

Detail pane

Field List

Toolbox

You can resize the Detail pane.
Move the mouse pointer over a side or corner (the pointer changes to a 4-pronged arrow). Click and drag appropriately. Release the button to confirm the operation.

The Detail pane – see below – represents the current body of your form. Here, you create and design the necessary fields.

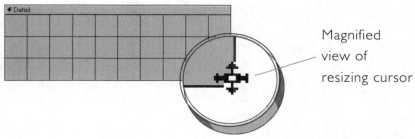

Magnified view of resizing cursor

AutoFormat

Access provides a way to apply a series of pre-defined formats to overall form design. Use AutoFormat to impose:

- a background

- a preset control font

- a preset control border

Using AutoFormat

Do the following to select the entire form:

Click here

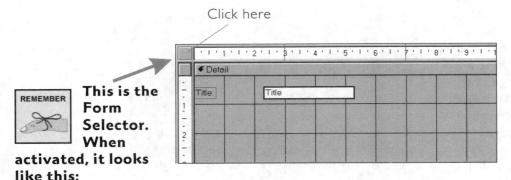

This is the Form Selector. When activated, it looks like this:

Now pull down the Format menu and click AutoFormat. Carry out the following steps:

Double-click a style

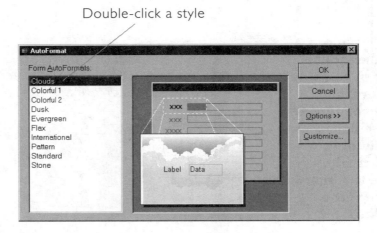

Adding labels (1)

HANDY TIP **If the form header/ footer area isn't currently visible, pull down the View menu and click Form Header/ Footer.**

It's useful to add descriptive labels to forms. You can add labels to:

- the form header or footer

- the Detail pane

First, refer to the Form toolbox and do the following:

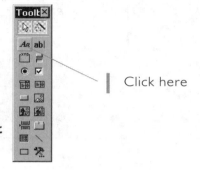

Click here

HANDY TIP **Re step 1 – in Access 95, the Toolbox toolbar is somewhat different. Click this button instead:**

Move the pointer to the appropriate location in the header/ footer or Detail pane. Hold down the left mouse button and drag to define the label area:

Label area

REMEMBER **This magnified view shows how the cursor changes when you're defining a label:**

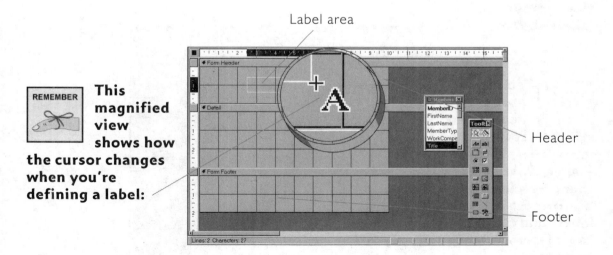

Header

Footer

Release the mouse button to complete the label.

Adding labels (2)

Access 97 users can add tabbed controls to forms.

Click this button:

in the Toolbox toolbar. In the form, click where you want the tabbed control to go. This is the result:

Now use the procedures on pages 67-69 to add the appropriate labels and/or fields.

So far, your label looks something like this:

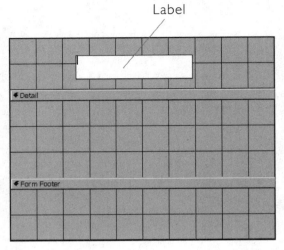

Label

The next stage is to type in the label text. When you've finished, press Enter.

You'll probably need to reformat most labels after you've created them. See the 'Reformatting labels and fields' topic later for how to do this.

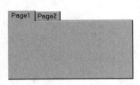

The inserted label

Adding fields

In Access 95, Design View was known as Form Design view.

Once you've inserted the necessary labels, the next stage is to insert the required fields. This is a simple process involving a drag-and-drop technique.

In Design View, make sure the Field List is visible. (If it isn't, pull down the View menu and click Field List.) Then do the following:

2 Drag it to the appropriate location in the form

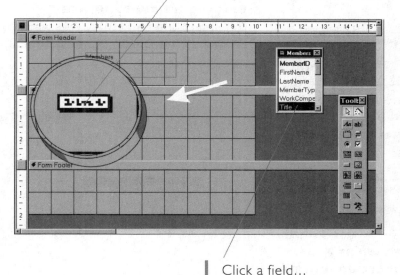

Click a field...

Fields in forms consist of two parts:
* **the field name:**

Title:

* **the field detail:**

Title

Release the mouse button to insert the new field.

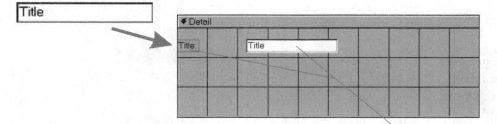

The new field

Reformatting labels and fields (1)

Once you've inserted a new label or field, you can:

- apply a new typeface and/or type size

- align the contents

- apply foreground and/or background colours

- specify a border width and/or colour

- apply special effects

You can select multiple controls by holding down Shift as you click them.

Applying a new typeface
First, select the control(s) you want to amend. Then refer to the Formatting (Form/Report) toolbar and do the following:

If you want to reformat the field name *as well as* the field detail, don't forget to select it, too.

Click here

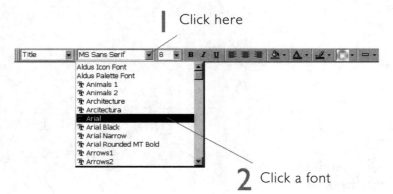

2 Click a font

In Access 95, the toolbar used here is known as the Formatting (Form/ Report Design) toolbar, and is slightly different.

Applying a new type size
First, select the control(s) you want to amend. Then do the following:

Click here

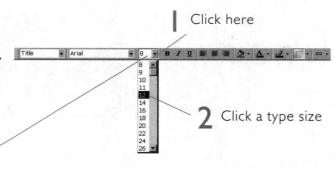

2 Click a type size

For greater precision, omit steps 1 and 2. Instead, type in a new type size here: Then press Return.

Reformatting labels and fields (2)

Aligning label and field contents

First, select the control you want to amend by clicking it. (If you want to select more than one, hold down Shift at the same time.) Then carry out any of the following:

The examples below show alignment in action:

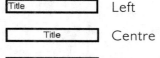

	Left
	Centre
	Right

2 Click here to centre control contents

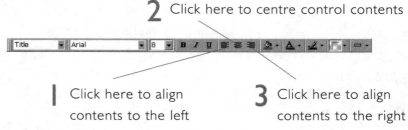

1 Click here to align contents to the left

3 Click here to align contents to the right

Colouring foregrounds and backgrounds

First, select the control you want to amend by clicking it. (If you want to select more than one, hold down Shift at the same time.) Then follow steps 1 AND 2 to apply a background colour, or 3 AND 4 to apply a foreground colour:

Re steps 1 and 3 – in Access 95, the toolbar buttons are slightly different:

 Foreground colour button

 Background colour button

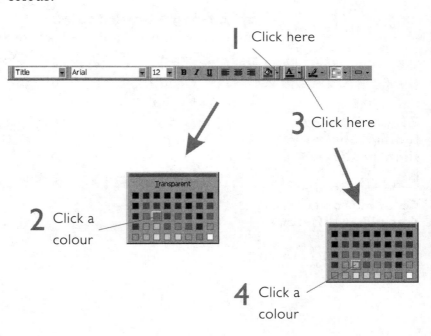

1 Click here

3 Click here

2 Click a colour

4 Click a colour

Reformatting labels and fields (3)

Specifying a border width

Access is supplied with a small number of pre-defined line widths which can be applied to controls. Note, however, that you can only apply the appropriate border to all four sides of a control: you can't specify which edges you border.

First, select the control you want to amend by clicking it. (If you want to select more than one, hold down Shift at the same time.) Then do the following:

 In Access 95, the Line/ Border Width button is slightly different:

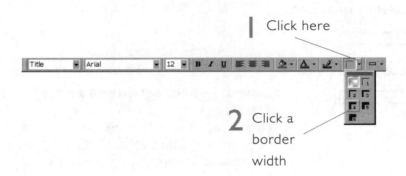

Click here

2 Click a border width

Specifying a border colour

First, select the control you want to amend by clicking it. (If you want to select more than one, hold down Shift at the same time.)

Then do the following:

 In Access 95, the Line/ Border Color button is somewhat different:

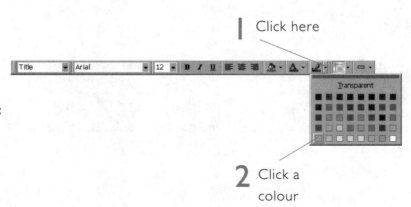

Click here

2 Click a colour

Reformatting labels and fields (4)

Applying special effects

Access lets you apply several special effects to controls. For instance, you can choose from:

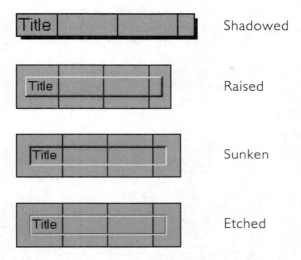

Shadowed

Raised

Sunken

Etched

First, select the control you want to amend by clicking it. (If you want to select more than one, hold down Shift at the same time.) Then do the following:

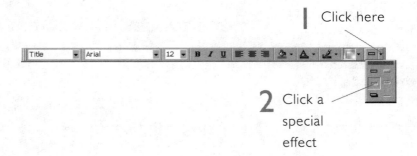

Click here

2 Click a special effect

Saving your form design

When you've finished designing your form, it's necessary to save your work to disk. This is a two-stage process and involves:

- closing down your form

- responding appropriately to a warning message

Do the following:

 To avoid data loss, you should also save your work *on-the-fly*. To do this, simply press Ctrl+S at frequent intervals.

Click here

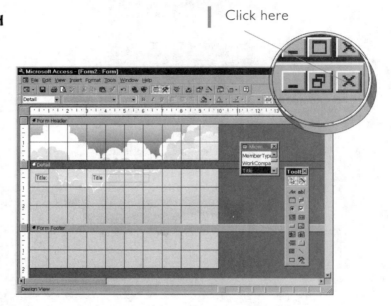

 Access 97 users – for how to export forms onto the World Wide Web, see page 34.

2 Click here

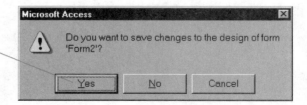

Chapter Five

Viewing and editing data

This chapter shows you how to interact with your data in Access views. Then you'll learn how to insert/delete records, find your way around in databases, and amend existing data. You'll search for specific data, sort it alphanumerically and then insert and use hyperlinks. Finally, you'll learn how to filter databases and save your filter to disk.

Covers

Using views – an overview

In Access 95, Design View was known as Form Design view.

Unlike forms, tables are only subject to two views:

- Datasheet view
- Design view (Table Design view in Access 95)

The comments under the 'Datasheet view' heading apply equally to forms and tables.

In Chapter 4, we looked at how to create and customise forms in Design View. Forms are, however, subject to two further views:

Datasheet view

Datasheet view presents your data in a grid structure reminiscent of a typical spreadsheet, with the columns denoting fields and the rows individual records. In Datasheet view, you can view more than one record at a time.

Use Datasheet view for bulk data entry or comparison.

Form view

Form view limits the display to one record at a time, while presenting it in a way which is more visual and therefore easier on the eye. The basis of this view is the 'form', the underlying database layout which you can customise in Design view (see Chapter 4).

In many circumstances, Form view provides the best way to interact with your database.

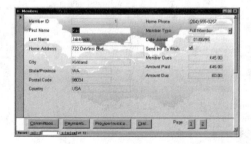

A form in Form view...

...and in Datasheet view

Switching between views

You can use two methods to switch to another view.

The menu approach
Pull down the View menu and do the following:

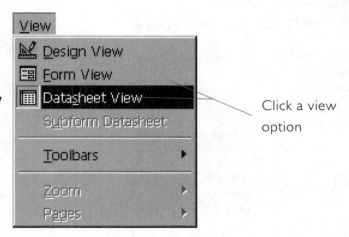

Click a view option

This is how the View menu appears if launched when a form is active. If you invoke it from within a table, however, there are only two view options to choose from:
- Design View and Datasheet View (in Access 97)
- Table Design View and Datasheet view (in Access 95)

The toolbar approach
Refer to the Form View toolbar (it displays automatically in both Form and Datasheet views).

Do the following:

Click here

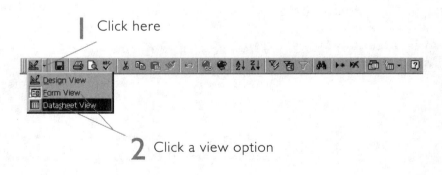

2 Click a view option

Inserting a new record

The procedures for entering data are very similar in both Datasheet and Form views.
N.ß. On this and future pages, the term 'Datasheet view' refers to both forms and tables.

Before we can go on to discuss techniques for entering data into Access databases, we need (since this is a necessary prerequisite) to deal with how to create a new record.

You can insert a new record in various ways.

The menu route
In either Datasheet or Form view, pull down the Insert menu and do the following:

Click here

Access 95 users should click Record in the Insert menu.

The toolbar route
In either Datasheet or Form view, refer to the Form View toolbar. Do the following:

Click here

In Access 95, the design of the Form View toolbar is slightly different.

The Record Gauge route
In Form view or Datasheet view, refer to the Record Gauge in the bottom left-hand corner of the screen. Do the following:

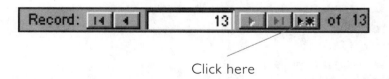

Click here

Entering data

When you've created a new record, Access places the insertion point in the first appropriate field:

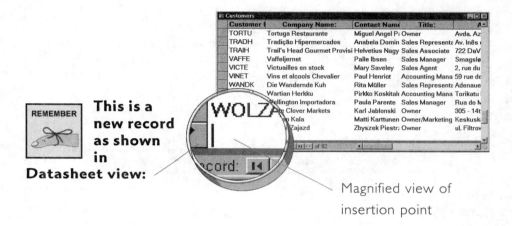

 This is a new record as shown in Datasheet view:

Magnified view of insertion point

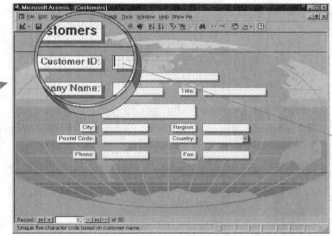

This is a new record as shown in Form view.

Magnified view of insertion point

 Instead of pressing Enter, you can also press Tab.

Whichever view you're using, type in the necessary data and press Enter; Access moves the insertion point to the next field. Repeat the above procedure, as necessary. If you don't want to enter data in a field, press Enter as often as necessary until the insertion point is in a field you do want to insert data into.

Database navigation (1)

Access makes it easy to move around in databases. The techniques for doing this are almost identical whether you're using Datasheet or Form views.

Using the Record Gauge

Press F5 to have Access place the insertion point in the Record Gauge. Then click any of the following locations to produce the specified effect:

To first record   To last record

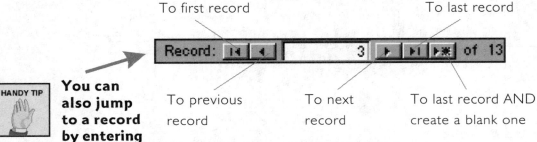

To previous   To next   To last record AND
record   record   create a blank one

You can also jump to a record by entering its number here:

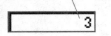

and pressing Enter.

Using keyboard shortcuts

The following keystroke combinations can be used to move around in both Datasheet and Form views:

End	Moves to the last field in the current record
Home	Moves to the first field in the current record
Ctrl+End	Moves to the last field in the last record
Ctrl+Home	Moves to the first field in the first record
↑	(In Datasheet view and tables only) Goes to the active field in the previous record
↓	(In Datasheet view and tables only) Goes to the active field in the next record

BEWARE
In Form view, ↑ moves to the previous field in the same record, and ↓ takes you to the next field in the same record.

Database navigation (2)

In Form view, Page Up and Page Down are subject to a proviso. When the start or end of the current record has been reached, Access moves to the previous or next record, respectively.

Ctrl+↑	Moves to the active field in the first record
Ctrl+↓	Moves to the active field in the last record
Page Up	Moves up by one screen
Page Down	Moves down by one screen
F5	Places the insertion point in the Record Gauge. (See the 'Using the Record Gauge' section opposite for how to use this.)
Ctrl+Page Up	(In Datasheet view) Moves one screen to the left
Ctrl+Page Down	(In Datasheet view) Moves one screen to the right

In Form view, Ctrl+Page Up takes you to the previous record, and Ctrl+Page Down to the next.

Using the scroll bars

In Datasheet view, you can use the horizontal scroll bar to move through fields which aren't currently visible. The vertical scroll bar moves through records which are currently off-screen:

As with all Windows programs, Access only displays scroll bars if the contents of a window are too large to display in their entirety.

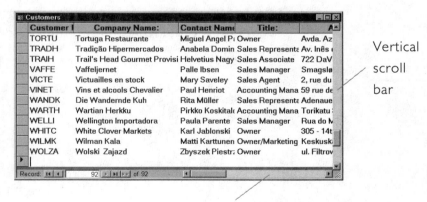

Vertical scroll bar

Horizontal scroll bar

In Form view, the scroll bars move you to hidden areas of the current record.

Amending data (1)

To edit existing database data, click the appropriate field in the relevant record (this applies to both Datasheet and Form views). One of two things happens now:

- if the field is empty, you can begin typing in data immediately

- if the field already contains data, Access highlights it:

First Name

Karl

Simply begin typing; Access automatically overwrites the existing data.

Entering Navigation mode

You can use Navigation mode in Form and Datasheet views.

Access has a special mode which lets you move around *within* fields. Navigation mode is useful (even essential) if the field contents are extensive.

When Navigation mode is active, the various keystroke combinations work as they would normally in respect of text entry in a word processor. For example, the up and down cursor keys move the insertion point up or down within the field (rather than to the previous or next fields). Home moves the insertion point to the start of the current line, rather than taking it to the start of the current record; End takes it to the end of the current line, rather than taking it to the final field in the current record.

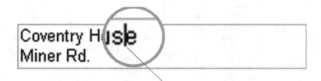

Coventry House
Miner Rd.

Magnified view of insertion point in Navigation mode

To enter Navigation mode, click a field and press F2. To return to data entry mode, press F2 again.

Amending data (2)

Access has another, particularly useful feature which you can use when the contents of a specific field exceed its width.

Using the Zoom box

The Zoom box is, in effect, a special editing window which displays the whole of a field's contents, however extensive.

The next illustration shows the field detail section of an address field in a database form:

> Brecon House
> Fifth Floor

You can use the Zoom box in Form and Datasheet views.

The address here consists of three lines, but only two display in the form. To view and/or edit the entire field, click in it. Then press Shift+F2. Now carry out the following steps:

| Type in replacement data, or click outside the highlighted text and make any necessary revisions

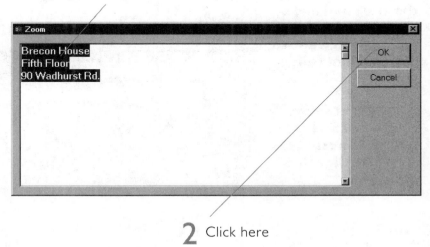

2 Click here

Deleting records

It's sometimes necessary to remove unwanted records from databases. Access makes this easy, in Datasheet or Form views.

In Form view, use the techniques listed in earlier topics to move to the record you want to delete. In forms or tables in Datasheet view, do the following:

This arrow (shown in a magnified view) is the record selector:

Click the appropriate entry in the Record header

You can only delete _multiple_ records in Datasheet view. Hold down Shift as you click the record headers at the start and end of the range of records you want to delete. Then follow step 1.

HANDY TIP
In Access 95, this message is slightly different.

Now pull down the Edit menu and click Delete Record. Access launches a warning message. Do one of the following:

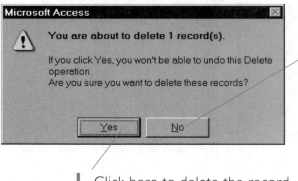

2 Click here to abort the deletion

Click here to delete the record

Using Undo

You can reverse many editing operations in Access. These include:

- saved changes to a record

- edits to field contents (e.g. deletions)

- all edits to the active record

The essential point to bear in mind is that you can only undo operations *if you haven't carried out any further actions of the type being undone.* For instance, if you alter and save the active record, you can only undo the amendments you've made before you edit another. If you revise the data in a field, you can only reverse this before leaving the field.

 You can also use keyboard shortcuts to undo actions. For example, to undo record operations press Esc. To undo record saves and changes to field contents, press Ctrl+Z.

Undoing the last operation
Pull down the Edit menu and do the following:

 In Access 95, the Edit menu is slightly different.

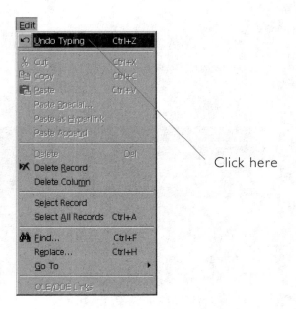

Click here

Note that the precise contents of the menu entry depend on the nature of the operation being undone.

Find operations

REMEMBER

For instance, a case-specific search for 'man' will not flag 'Man' or 'MAN'.

Access lets you search the active database for text and/or numbers. You can:

- search through all fields within every record, or limit the search to a specific field in every record

- search forwards or backwards, or through the whole database

- limit the search to exact matches (i.e. Access will only flag data which has the same upper- and lower-case make-up)

- limit the search to field sections (the beginning of fields, the whole field or any part)

REMEMBER

If you want to restrict the search to a specific field in every record, select the field *before* you launch the Edit menu. Then omit step 5 below.

Searching for data

Pull down the Edit menu and click Find. Now carry out step 1 below, then any of steps 2-5. Finally, carry out step 6 OR 7:

1 Type in the data you want to find

2 Click here to make the search case-specific

6 Click here to flag the first match

HANDY TIP

Re step 1 – you can also enter wildcards here:

? represents any 1 character
* represents any number of characters
For instance, searching for 'wh?le' will find 'whole', 'whale' or 'while', and 'wh?le*' will also locate 'wholesome'.

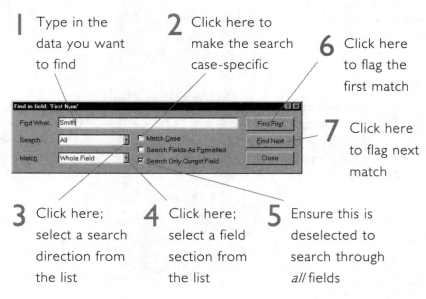

7 Click here to flag next match

3 Click here; select a search direction from the list

4 Click here; select a field section from the list

5 Ensure this is deselected to search through *all* fields

Find-and-replace operations

When you search for data you can also – if you want – have Access replace it with something else. You can:

- search through all fields within every record, or limit the search to a specific field in every record

- search forwards or backwards, or through the whole database

- limit the search to exact matches (i.e. Access will only flag data which has the same upper- and lower-case make-up)

Replacing data

Pull down the Edit menu and click Replace. Carry out steps 1-2 below, then any of 3-5. Now do *one* of the following:

- Follow step 6. When Access locates the first search target, carry out step 7 to have it replaced. Repeat as often as required

- Carry out step 8 to have every target replaced automatically

If you want to restrict the search to a specific field in every record, select the field *before* you launch the Edit menu. Then omit step 5 below.

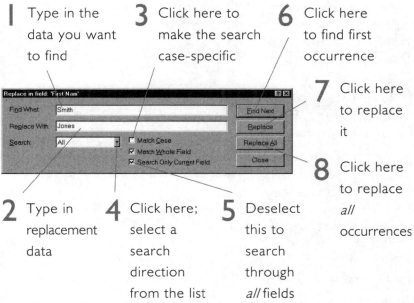

| Type in the data you want to find

3 Click here to make the search case-specific

6 Click here to find first occurrence

7 Click here to replace it

8 Click here to replace *all* occurrences

2 Type in replacement data

4 Click here; select a search direction from the list

5 Deselect this to search through *all* fields

Sorting data

Find operations locate specific records based on one specified criterion. However, Access lets you take this a stage further. You can have records arranged in a specific order; this is called 'sorting'. Sorting your data often helps you find information more quickly, in both tables and forms. You can sort data in ascending order, with the following level of priority:

*   0 to 9

then

*   A to Z

You can also sort data in descending order (9 to 0, Z to A).

Carrying out a sort

In either Datasheet or Form view, click the field on which you want to base the sort. Pull down the Records menu and click Sort, Ascending or Sort, Descending.

In forms and tables in Datasheet view, you can sort by more than one field (from the left). Simply select more than one column before you implement the sort.

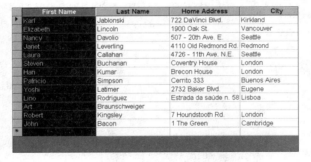

Before the sort, with the First Name field selected

First Name	Last Name	Home Address	City
Art	Braunschweiger		
Elizabeth	Lincoln	1900 Oak St.	Vancouver
Hari	Kumar	Brecon House	London
Janet	Leverling	4110 Old Redmond Rd.	Redmond
John	Bacon	1 The Green	Cambridge
Karl	Jablonski	722 DaVinci Blvd.	Kirkland
Laura	Callahan	4726 - 11th Ave. N.E.	Seattle
Lino	Rodriguez	Estrada da saúde n. 58	Lisboa
Nancy	Davolio	507 - 20th Ave. E.	Seattle
Patricio	Simpson	Cerrito 333	Buenos Aires
Robert	Kingsley	7 Houndstooth Rd.	London
Steven	Buchanan	Coventry House	London
Yoshi	Latimer	2732 Baker Blvd.	Eugene

After an ascending sort

To return your data to the way it was before a sort, pull down the Records menu and click Remove Filter/Sort.

Hyperlinks New in Access 97

You can use hyperlinks in tables or forms to jump to:

- another Access database

- a document on the Internet

Inserting a hyperlinked field into a table

Follow the procedures on page 45 to open the relevant table in Design view. Then follow steps 1-2 on page 46 to insert the new field. (In step 2, however, select Hyperlink). Go to Datasheet view; in the hyperlinked field entry which corresponds to the appropriate record, type in details of the specific hyperlink. See the illustration below for an example:

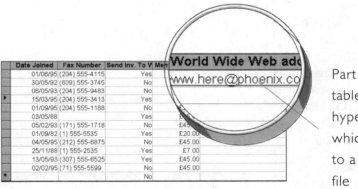

Date Joined	Fax Number	Send Inv. To W	Men
01/06/95	(204) 555-4115	Yes	
30/05/92	(609) 555-3745	No	
06/05/93	(204) 555-9483	No	
15/03/95	(204) 555-3413	Yes	
01/09/95	(204) 555-1188	No	
03/05/88		Yes	£45
05/02/93	(171) 555-1718	No	£45
01/09/82	(1) 555-5535	Yes	£20.00
04/05/95	(212) 555-6875	No	£45.00
25/11/88	(1) 555-2535	Yes	£7.00
13/05/93	(307) 555-6525	Yes	£45.00
02/02/95	(71) 555-5599	No	£45.00
*		No	

World Wide Web add
www.here@phoenix.co

Part of a table hyperlink which jumps to a Web file

HANDY TIP

To use a hyperlink in a form, ensure you're in Form view. Move the mouse pointer over the hyperlink:

This jumps

`db1.mdb` to an Access

database

The cursor changes to a pointing hand. Left-click once.

Using a hyperlink in a table

Ensure you're in Datasheet view. Move the mouse pointer over the entry you want to jump to (the cursor changes to a pointing hand). Left-click once.

Inserting a hyperlink into a form

First, follow the procedures on page 64 to open the relevant form in Design view. Then click this button – 🖳 – in the Form Design toolbar. In the 'Link to file or URL:' field in the Insert Hyperlink dialog, type in the address of the file or Internet site you want to jump to. Click OK. Access inserts the relevant hyperlink.

Move and/or resize this using standard Windows techniques.

Filtering data (1)

Sorting data is one way of customising the way it displays on screen. Another method you can use is 'filtering'. When you apply a filter, Access hides records which don't match the requirements ('criteria') you set.

Filtering involves:

- selecting the fields through which Access should search

- specifying the sort order (one particular advantage to filtering is that you can apply differing sort orders to the various fields)

- specifying what the fields must contain (criteria) to have their records display

- applying the filter

Setting up a filter

In Datasheet or Form view, pull down the Records menu and click Filter, Advanced Filter/Sort. Do the following:

 Repeat steps 1-4 for as many fields as you want to include in the filter.
   Note that Access may pre-select a field and insert it in the first column. If this isn't what you want, click the arrow to the right of the Field box:

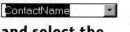

and select the correct field from the list. Then follow steps 2-4.

 Re step 4 – criteria are usually simple to use. For example, in the example shown, the first field pulls in records whose First Name is John.

Double-click a field

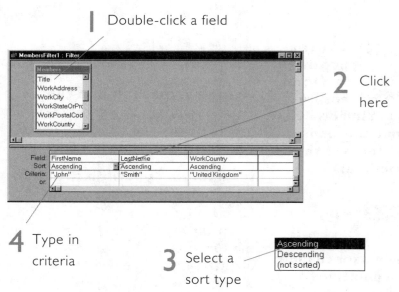

2 Click here

4 Type in criteria

3 Select a sort type

Ascending
Descending
(not sorted)

Filtering data (2)

HANDY TIP

In Access 95, the Filter/Sort toolbar is slightly different.

Applying a filter

Once you've set up a filter, the next stage is to implement it. You can use the Filter/Sort toolbar (a special toolbar which launches automatically when you set up a filter) to do this.

Do the following:

Click here

REMEMBER

When you filter data, the effects are only temporary: the underlying table is unaffected.

The illustration below shows a filtered database in Datasheet view:

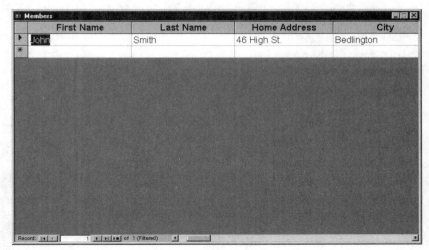

First Name	Last Name	Home Address	City
John	Smith	46 High St.	Bedlington

HANDY TIP

Another way to remove a filter is to click this button:

in the Form View toolbar, *after* you've closed the Filter dialog.

Removing the filter

When you've finished with a filter, you can deactivate it.

First, close the active Filter dialog by pressing Ctrl+F4. Then pull down the Records menu and click Remove Filter/Sort.

Saving/opening filters

When you close the Filter dialog (or Access itself), details of any filter you've set up are lost. If you plan to use a filter again, however, you can save it to disk.

Access regards filters as queries. For how to work with queries, see Chapter 6.

Saving a filter
With the Filter dialog still open, pull down the File menu and click Save As Query. Do the following:

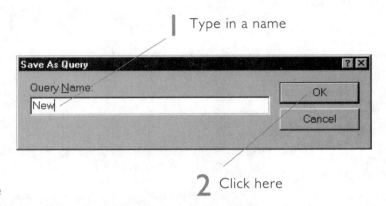

Type in a name

2 Click here

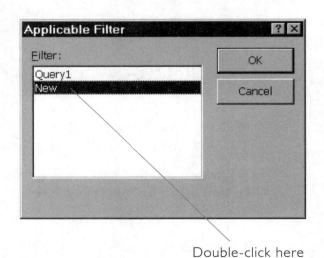
Saved filters appear as queries under the Queries tab in the Database window.

Reopening a filter
To work with a filter you've already set up, make sure the Filter dialog is open. Pull down the File menu and click Load From Query. Do the following:

Double-click here

Querying databases

This chapter shows you how to retrieve highly specific information from your databases with the use of sophisticated queries. You'll learn how to create queries rapidly and easily with wizards, and apply them automatically. Then you'll create queries *manually*, for more precision. Finally, you'll save your manual query to disk, and then discover how to open and apply it.

Covers

Chapter Six

Queries – an overview

In Chapter 5, we looked at ways to enter data into databases. However, a large part of database use consists of *extracting* information. The trick is to get precisely the information you need, in the right format. Queries represent a highly accurate and useful way of doing this.

When you set up and institute a query, you 'interrogate' the active database; the result – the 'answer' – can then be viewed on screen, or even printed. At the same time, the information which does not satisfy the criteria you set is conveniently ignored, although of course it still remains within the database. The ability to (in effect) hide information is what makes queries so indispensable.

The main types of query are:

Select queries   These extract information from tables, based on the criteria you specify. Select queries are the most frequent type, and the Access default.

Crosstab queries   These use criteria you set to summarise table data in a spreadsheet format. Crosstab queries are the most complex to use, but arguably the most useful.

Query creation

You can create queries in two ways:

•   with Query Wizards

•   manually

There are four Query Wizards; we'll examine two (the Simple Query and Crosstab Query Wizards) in some detail in this chapter.

We'll also look at manual query creation.

The Simple Query Wizard (1)

Use the Simple Query Wizard to create a Select query.

First, make sure the Database window is visible (see page 37 in Chapter 3 for how to do this). Then do the following:

Click here

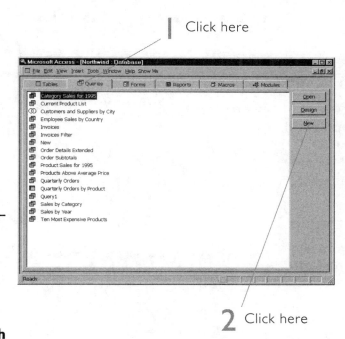

REMEMBER

Re step 3 – **you can run two other wizards here. The Find Duplicates Query Wizard locates records with duplicated field values in any one table; the Find Unmatched Query Wizard compares tables and isolates records which are unrelated.**
To run either of these, simply double-click the relevant entry and follow the on-screen instructions.

2 Click here

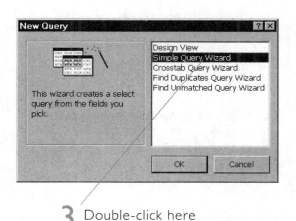

3 Double-click here

The Simple Query Wizard (2)

Now carry out the following steps:

Click here; select a table in the list

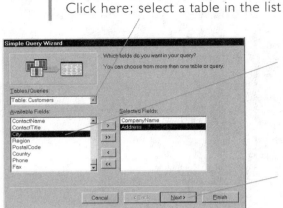

2 Double-click the field(s) you want to include in the query

HANDY TIP

Re step 1 – if you want to use fields from an additional table, click here:

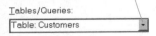

Tables/Queries:

Table: Customers

Then select a new table from the list. Finally, repeat step 2 as often as necessary.
  When you've specified enough fields, follow steps 3-6.

3 Click here

4 Name the query

5 Click here to open the new query after step 6

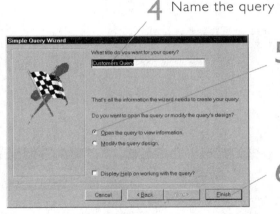

6 Click here

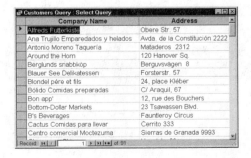

The resulting query

The Crosstab Query Wizard (1)

Crosstab queries summarise data from the fields you specify, and present it in a convenient tabular form.

First, make sure the Database window is visible (see page 37 in Chapter 3 for how to do this). Then do the following:

Click here

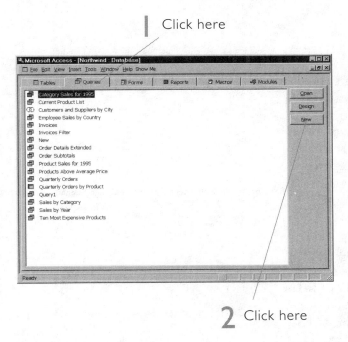

2 Click here

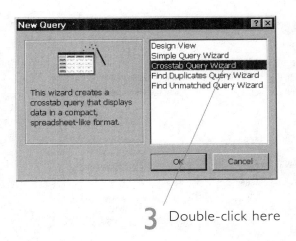

3 Double-click here

The Crosstab Query Wizard (2)

HANDY TIP

Access 95 users should omit steps 1-3: this dialog does not appear.

Now carry out the following steps:

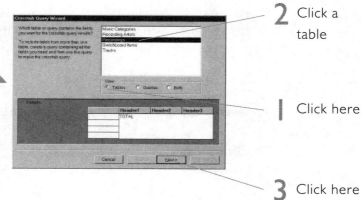

2 Click a table

1 Click here

3 Click here

REMEMBER

In this example, we take two fields from a database created with the MUSIC COLLECTION Wizard:

- Recording Title
- Recording Artist ID

Then we instruct the wizard – in later dialogs – to correlate the total number of tracks (the 'correlation field') in each title against the appropriate Artist ID number...

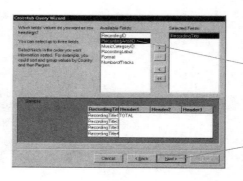

4 Double-click up to 3 fields

5 Click here

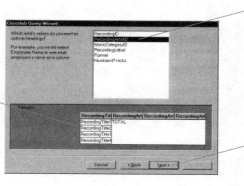

6 Click the field you want to serve as the column heading

HANDY TIP

This section previews your selected fields.

7 Click here

The Crosstab Query Wizard (3)

Complete the query, as follows:

1 Click a correlation field (see the Remember tip on page 98)

(see the Remember tip on page 98)

HANDY TIP

Access previews the resultant query here:

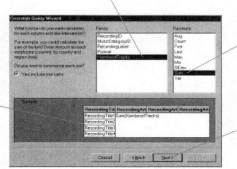

2 Click a calculation type

3 Click here

4 Name the query

5 Click here to open the new query after step 6

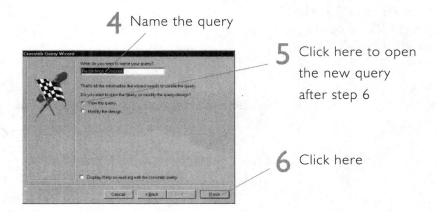

6 Click here

This is the result:

Artists' ID numbers

Recording Title	Total Of NumberofTracks	1	2	3
Look Both Ways	12		12	
Meditations	6			
Noise in the Garage	10		10	
Opus 65	5	5		
Outback	10		10	
Short Circuit	7			7
Sounds Better Louder	10		10	

Individual track totals

Creating a query manually (1)

There are two ways to begin query creation manually.

HANDY TIP

Re step 2 – Access 95 users should click New Query.

REMEMBER

This happens to be the Form View toolbar. However, the New Object button is in nearly every toolbar.
In Access 95, the Form View toolbar is slightly different.

Using the New Object button
Do the following:

Click here

2 Click here

AutoForm
AutoReport
Table
Query
Form
Report
Macro
Module
Class Module

Using the Database window
Alternatively, make sure the Database window is visible (see page 37 for how to do this). Then do the following:

Click here

2 Click here

Creating a query manually (2)

Now carry out the following steps:

1 Click here

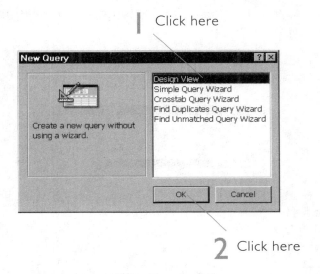

2 Click here

This is the result:

Query Design window

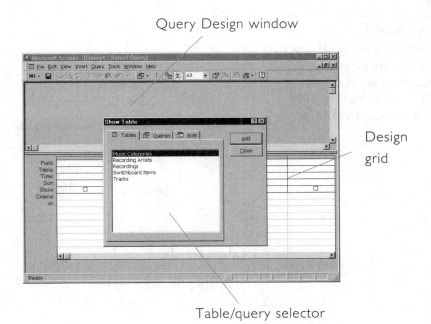

Design grid

Table/query selector

Creating a query manually (3)

The next stage is to select the tables (and/or existing queries) which contain the fields you want to insert into your query. Do the following, repeating step 2 as often as necessary:

Ensure this tab is active

REMEMBER

This is a magnified view of a 'join line'. Access establishes join lines when it detects that two fields have the same name and data type (and when one is a primary key). If no join lines are established, you have to rectify this – see page 103:

Show Table

| Tables | Queries | Both |

Music Categories
Recording Artists
Recordings
Recordings_Crosstab
Switchboard Items
Tracks

Add
Close

3 Click here

2 Double-click the tables/queries you want to include

After step 2, Access launches Field lists displaying available fields:

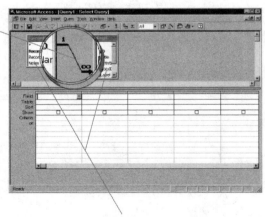

Field lists

Creating a query manually (4)

The next stage is to join tables in the Design window if:

- you have more than one Field list in the window

- the Field lists relate to tables (they probably will)

- Access hasn't already created an automatic join (see the Remember tip on page 102 for more information on this)

Do the following:

REMEMBER **The zoomed area shows the transformation in the mouse pointer while you create the join.**

Click a field; drag it to its counterpart in the second table

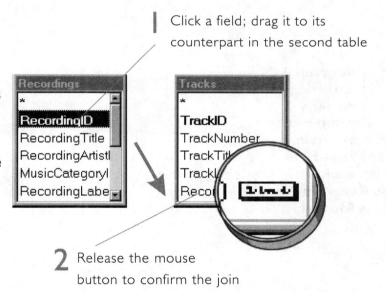

2 Release the mouse button to confirm the join

The illustration below shows the completed join:

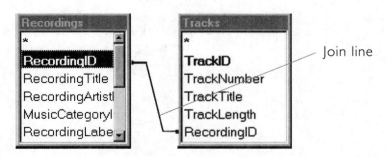

Join line

Creating a query manually (5)

Now carry out the following steps:

HANDY TIP

Re step 1 – as you **double-click** *subsequent* fields, **Access inserts them in adjacent columns in the Design grid.**

REMEMBER

Re step 4 – criteria are usually simple to use. For example, here the first field pulls in records whose **Recording Artist is Mozart.**

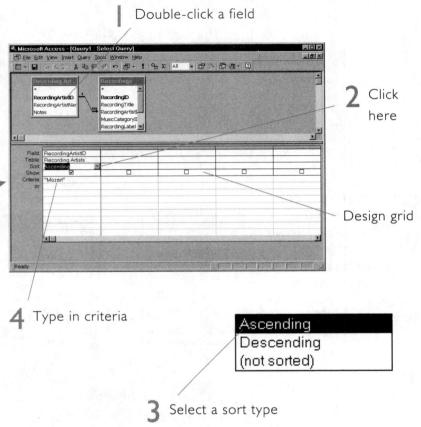

Double-click a field

2 Click here

Design grid

4 Type in criteria

Ascending
Descending
(not sorted)

3 Select a sort type

Repeat steps 1-4 for as many fields (using all the relevant Field lists in the Query Design window) as you want to include in the query.

The final stage in creating a manual query is to save it to disk for future use. See page 105 how to do this.

Refer to page 106 for how to apply manual queries.

Saving your query

Manually generated queries need to be saved to disk for later use.

You can also use the procedures outlined in this topic to save existing queries under a new name.

Saving a query

With the Query Design window still open, pull down the File menu and do the following:

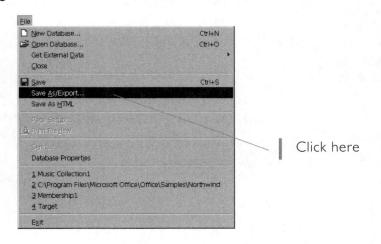

Click here

In Access 95, the File menu is slightly different.

2 Click here

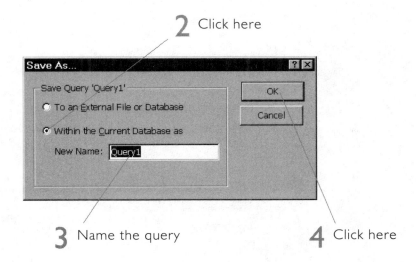

3 Name the query

4 Click here

Applying/opening queries

 You can also apply a query directly from within the Query Design window. Simply pull down the Query menu and click Run.

HANDY TIP

When you open a manual query you've previously saved to disk, Access applies it to your data. (Note, however, that queries created with a wizard are automatically opened and applied at the end of the creation process – see earlier topics for more information on this.)

Opening/applying a query

First, ensure the Database window is visible (for how to do this, see page 37 in Chapter 3). Now do the following:

Activate the Queries tab

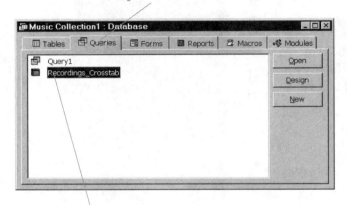

2 Double-click the query you want to open

Closing down a query

In any open query, do the following:

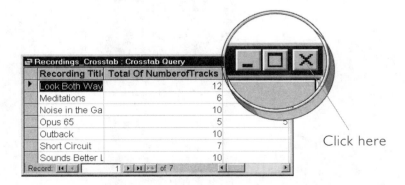

Click here

Creating reports

This chapter shows you how to view your data as reports. You'll learn how to create straightforward reports with AutoReports. You'll also build more complex reports with the Report Wizard; create reports *manually*, for more precision; and discover how to customise the way report components display. Finally, you'll save your manually generated reports to disk (and – for Access 97 users – to the Internet) and then view them.

Chapter Seven

Reports – an overview

In Chapter 4, we looked at the creation and use of database forms. Forms allow you to enter data in a user-friendly way. Reports have a similar effect on the way you view (and print) data. When you create and view a report, however, you have:

- more control over the layout

- the ability to customise the printed output (see Chapter 9 for more information on printing reports)

Before you set up and institute a report, you should do the following:

HANDY TIP

Reports can be based on either tables or queries; or instances of both.

- examine your database, taking account of the current tables, forms and queries

- be clear in your own mind which components of your database represent data, and make sure you've entered all the data you want reports to display

- if you want to enter data *as well as* view it, use a form (you can't enter information into reports)

- if you've created previous reports (or if you've used a wizard to create a database and reports have been created automatically in the process, as is normally the case), review them with a view to highlighting areas which need improving.

Report creation

You can create reports in two ways:

- with Report Wizards/AutoReports

- manually

There are three main Report Wizards/AutoReports; we'll examine these in later topics.

We'll also look at manual report creation.

Report Wizards

The three principal wizards are:

Columnar AutoReport	Automatically creates a quick, simple report for the selected table in a single column
Tabular AutoReport	Automatically creates a quick, simple report for the selected table in a tabular format
Report Wizard	Provides full control over which tables and fields are included, and extensive customisation

The AutoReports are an especially quick and convenient way to create reports. Use the Report Wizard when you need greater precision.

Columnar
AutoReport

Tabular
AutoReport

Creating AutoReport reports

First, make sure the Database window is visible (see Chapter 3 for how to do this). Now carry out the following steps:

Re step 5 – Access provides an extra Report Wizard: the Label Wizard. This creates reports which produce highly customisable labels in various formats.

To run the Label Wizard, simply double-click its name in the New Report dialog box: and follow the on-screen instructions.

1 Ensure the Reports tab is active

2 Click here

5 Click an AutoReport option

```
New Report                                    ? X

                      Design View
                      Report Wizard
   [icon]             AutoReport:  Columnar
                      AutoReport:  Tabular
                      Chart Wizard
   This wizard automatically    Label Wizard
   creates a columnar report.


   Choose the table or query
   where the object's data comes          [        ▼]
   from:

            OK           Cancel
```

3 Click here

After step 6, Access generates the AutoReport report.

6 Click here

```
CommitteeMembers
Committees
Members
Members Query
MemberTypes
My Organization Information
New
Payment Methods
Payments
Payments_Crosstab1
```

4 Click a table or query

Using the Report Wizard (1)

First, make sure the Database window is visible (see page 37 for how to do this). Now carry out the following steps:

Ensure the Reports tab is active

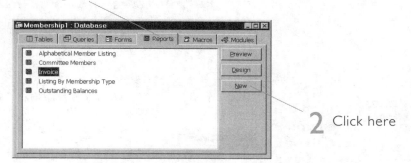

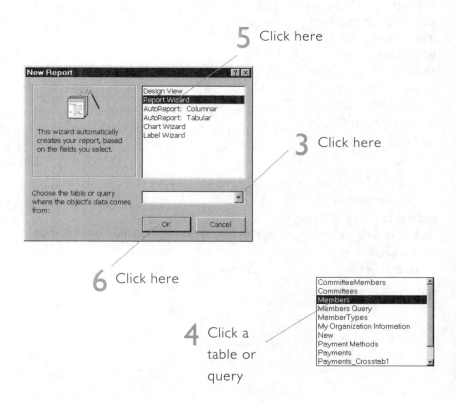

2 Click here

5 Click here

3 Click here

6 Click here

4 Click a table or query

Using the Report Wizard (2)

Now carry out the following steps:

Double-click the field(s) you want to include

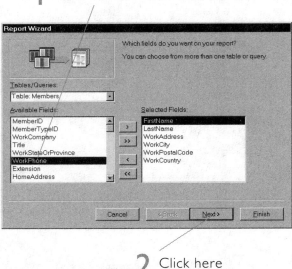

REMEMBER **Re step 1 – when you carried out steps 3 and 4 on page 111, you selected a table or query on which to base your new report. If you want to use fields from an *additional* table and/or query, click here:**

Tables/Queries:

| Table: Customers |

Then make a selection from the list. Finally, carry out steps 2-4, as appropriate.

2 Click here

In the next dialog, if any of the fields can be grouped under a convenient heading (this makes reports easier to follow), carry out steps 3 and 4 below (if not, simply follow step 4):

3 Double-click the heading field

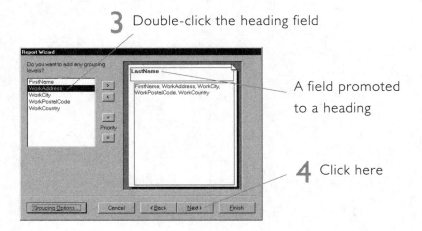

A field promoted to a heading

4 Click here

Using the Report Wizard (3)

If you followed steps 3 AND 4 on page 112, you now allocate sort fields for 'detail records' (those organised under group headings); if, on the other hand, you defined no headings, you sort *all* records here.

In the next dialog you can select up to four sort fields as a basis for ordering records. Carry out steps 1-3 below (to allocate more than one sort field, repeat steps 1-2 for fields below the first, THEN follow 3). Finally, follow steps 4-6.

Click here

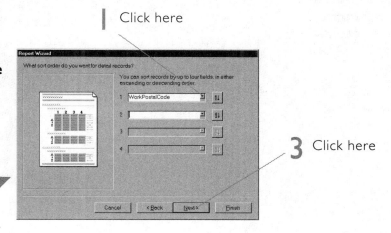

3 Click here

HANDY TIP

Click the button to the right of each sort field:

2 Click a field

| | Ascending |
| | Descending |

to toggle between Ascending or Descending sorts.

4 Choose a report layout

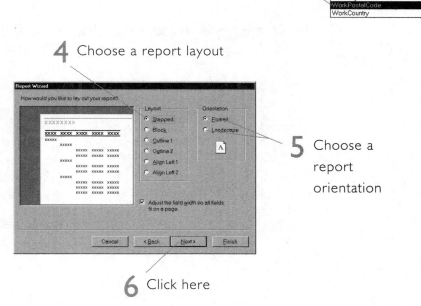

5 Choose a report orientation

6 Click here

Using the Report Wizard (4)

Now carry out the following steps:

Select a report style

HANDY TIP **Access previews report styles here:**

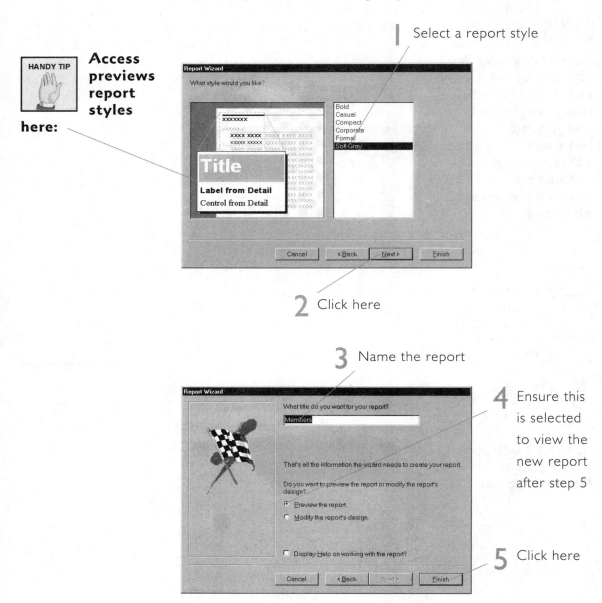

2 Click here

3 Name the report

4 Ensure this is selected to view the new report after step 5

5 Click here

Creating reports manually (1)

There are two ways to begin report creation manually.

Re step 2 –
Access 95
users
should
click New Report.

Using the New Object button
Do the following:

Click here

2 Click here

REMEMBER **This**
happens to
be the
Form View
toolbar. However,
the New Object
button is in nearly
every toolbar.
N.B. In Access 95,
the Form View
toolbar is slightly
different.

Using the Database window
Alternatively, make sure the Database window is visible (see page 37 in Chapter 3 for how to do this). Then do the following:

Ensure the Reports tab is active

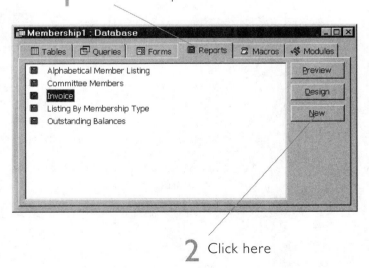

2 Click here

Creating reports manually (2)

Now carry out the following steps:

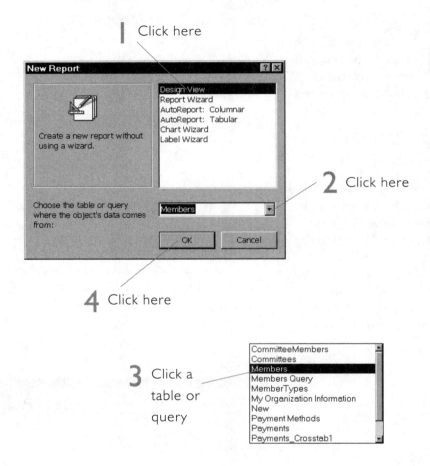

Click here

2 Click here

4 Click here

3 Click a
table or
query

After step 4, Access creates a blank report.

See the 'Amending report design' topics later (and others)
for how to customise it.

Report design – an overview

HANDY TIP **If you want to, you can also opt to** *redesign* **reports created with the various wizards.**

HANDY TIP **To see what your work looks like at any stage in the report design process, pull down the View menu and click Print Preview. To close the Preview window when you've finished with it, press Esc.**

Now that you've created a report manually, you need to add the various fields and labels (explanatory text). As with forms, Access calls everything you add to a report a 'control'. There are two main types:

• bound

• unbound

Bound controls pull in data from fields in an underlying database table or query. For instance, if a field in a table contains Address information, the relevant control will return location data for the currently active record.

Unbound controls, on the other hand, contain supplementary text (e.g. instructions to the database user) or graphics components (e.g. lines); they aren't connected to table fields.

The illustration below shows an excerpt from a previewed report:

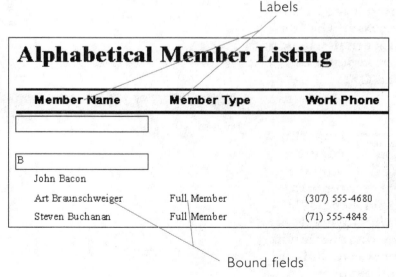

Labels

Alphabetical Member Listing

Member Name	Member Type	Work Phone
B		
John Bacon		
Art Braunschweiger	Full Member	(307) 555-4680
Steven Buchanan	Full Member	(71) 555-4848

Bound fields

Amending report design (1)

HANDY TIP

Access 97 users can add hyperlinks (see page 89 for a definition) **to their reports.**

To insert a hyperlink, follow the appropriate procedures here to open the report in Design view. Then click this button:

in the Report Design toolbar. In the 'Link to file or URL:' field in the Insert Hyperlink dialog, type in the address of the file or Internet site you want to jump to. Click OK.

BEWARE

Hyperlinks do not operate in reports *within Access 97 itself.* **However, they do function in reports which have been exported to HTML format (see page 127).**

There are two ways to begin customising a report's design.

If the report is already open

Pull down the View menu. Then, if you're an Access 97 user, do the following (Access 95 users should click Report Design in the View menu):

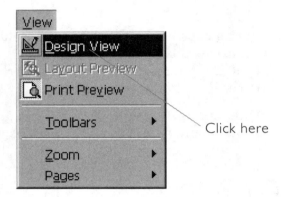

Click here

If the report isn't already open

Go to the Database window (see page 37 in Chapter 3 for how to do this) and do the following:

Ensure the Reports tab is active

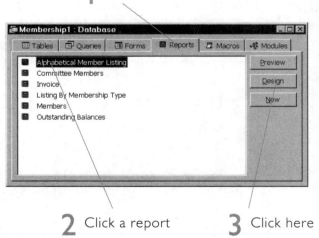

2 Click a report   **3** Click here

Amending report design (2)

REMEMBER

If you've just created a manual report, you'll already be in Design view.

Access now launches the report in Design view. This is the basis for adding and customising fields. The following components are especially important:

- the Detail pane
- the Toolbox
- the Field List

HANDY TIP

If the Field List isn't currently visible, pull down the View menu and click Field List.

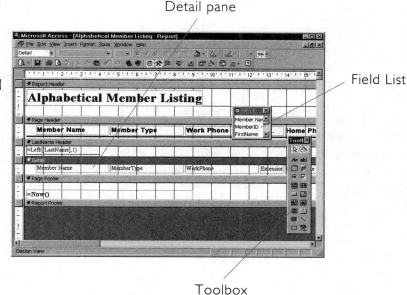

Detail pane

Field List

Toolbox

HANDY TIP

You can resize the Detail pane.

Move the mouse pointer over a side or corner (the pointer changes to a 4-pronged arrow). Click and drag appropriately. Release the button to confirm the operation.

The Detail pane represents the current body of your report. Here, you create and design the necessary fields.

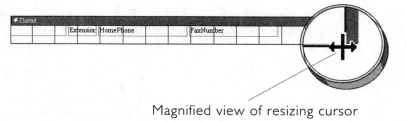

Magnified view of resizing cursor

AutoFormat

You can apply a series of pre-defined formats to overall report design. Use AutoFormat to impose:

- a background

- a preset control font

- a preset control border

Using AutoFormat

Do the following to select the entire report:

Click here

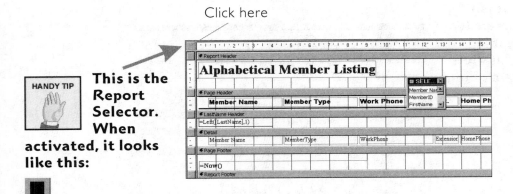

HANDY TIP

This is the Report Selector. When activated, it looks like this:

Now pull down the Format menu and click AutoFormat. Do the following:

Double-click a style

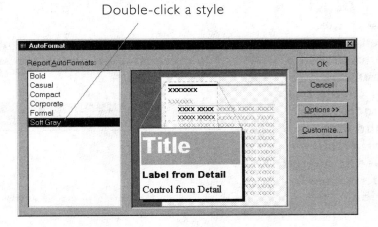

Adding labels (1)

Unlike forms, Access reports automatically display header and footer areas.

It's useful to add descriptive labels to reports. Report areas you can add labels to include:

- the report header or footer

- the Detail pane

First, refer to the Toolbox toolbar and do the following:

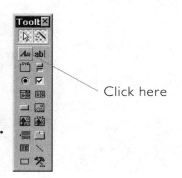

Click here

In Access 95, the Toolbox toolbar is somewhat different. Click this button, instead:

Move the pointer to the appropriate location in the header/footer or Detail pane. Hold down the left mouse button and drag to define the label area:

Label area

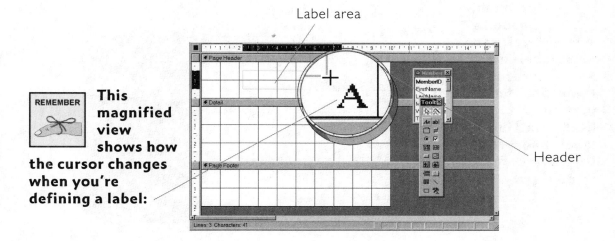

Header

This magnified view shows how the cursor changes when you're defining a label:

Release the mouse button to complete the first stage in label creation.

Adding labels (2)

So far, your label will look something like this:

Label

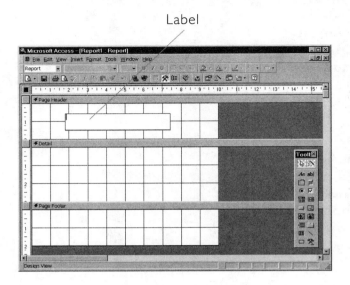

The next stage is to type in the label text. When you've finished, press Enter.

HANDY TIP
You'll probably need to reformat most labels after you've created them. See the various 'Reformatting labels and fields' topics later for how to do this.

The inserted (but not yet reformatted) label

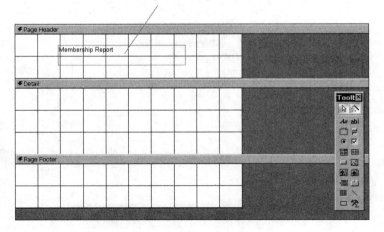

Adding fields

REMEMBER

In Access 95, Design View is known as Report Design.

Once you've inserted the necessary labels, the next stage is to insert the required fields. This is a simple process which involves a drag-and-drop technique.

In Design View, make sure the Field List is visible. (If it isn't, pull down the View menu and click Field List.) Then do the following:

2 Drag it to the appropriate location in the report

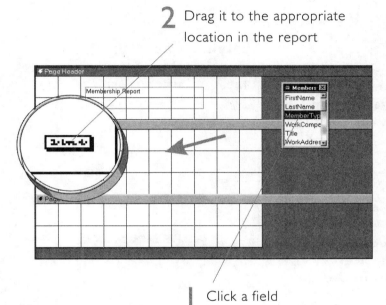

Click a field

Fields in reports consist of two parts:
- **the field name:**

Member Type

- **the field detail:**

MemberTypeID

Release the mouse button to insert the new field:

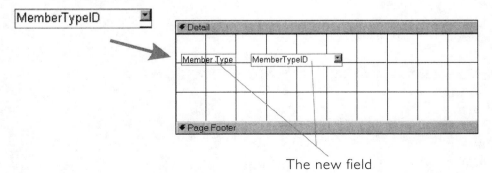

The new field

Reformatting labels and fields (1)

HANDY TIP

You can select multiple controls by holding down Shift as you click them.

REMEMBER

If you want to reformat the field name *as well as* the field detail, don't forget to select it as well.

REMEMBER

The toolbar shown here and on pages 125-126 is automatically present in Design View.
   In Access 95, it's known as the Formatting (Form/Report Design) toolbar, and is slightly different.

HANDY TIP

For greater precision, omit steps 1 and 2. Instead, type in a new type size here: Then press Return.

Once you've inserted a new label or field, you can:

- apply a new typeface

- apply a new type size

- align the contents

- apply foreground and/or background colours

- specify a border width and/or colour

Applying a new typeface

First, select the control(s) you want to amend. Then refer to the Formatting (Form/Report) toolbar and do the following:

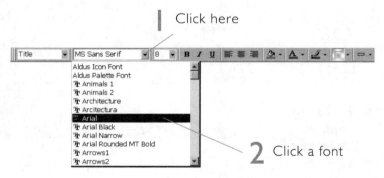

Click here

2 Click a font

Applying a new type size

First, select the control(s) you want to amend. Then do the following:

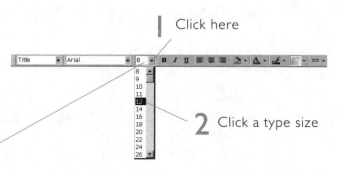

Click here

2 Click a type size

Reformatting labels and fields (2)

Aligning label and field contents

First, click the control you want to amend. (If you want to select more than one, hold down Shift at the same time.) Then carry out any of the following:

The examples below show alignment in action:

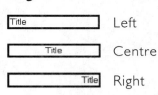

Left

Centre

Right

2 Click here to centre control contents

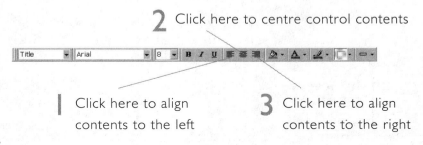

Click here to align contents to the left

3 Click here to align contents to the right

Colouring foregrounds and backgrounds

First, click the control you want to amend. (If you want to select more than one, hold down Shift at the same time.) Then follow steps 1 AND 2 to apply a background colour, or 3 AND 4 to apply a foreground colour:

Re steps 1 and 3 – in Access 95, the requisite toolbar buttons are slightly different:

 Background colour button

 Foreground colour button

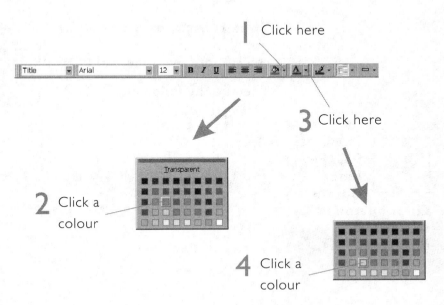

Click here

2 Click a colour

3 Click here

4 Click a colour

Reformatting labels and fields (3)

Specifying a border width

You can apply a small number of pre-defined line widths to controls. Note, however, that you can only apply the appropriate border to *all four sides* of a control: you can't specify which edges you border.

First, click the control you want to amend. (If you want to select more than one, hold down Shift at the same time.) Then do the following:

In Access 95, the Line/Border Width button is slightly different:

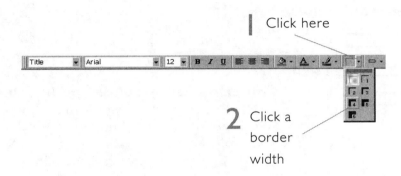

Click here

2 Click a border width

Specifying a border colour

First, click the control you want to amend. (If you want to select more than one, hold down Shift at the same time.)

Then do the following:

In Access 95, the Line/Border Color button is somewhat different:

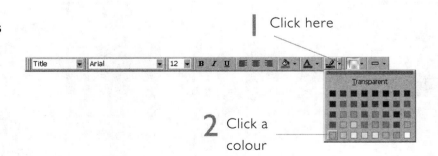

Click here

2 Click a colour

Saving your report

Manually generated reports need to be saved to disk for later use.

You can also use the procedures outlined in this topic to save existing reports under a new name.

Saving a report

Within Design view, pull down the File menu and do the following:

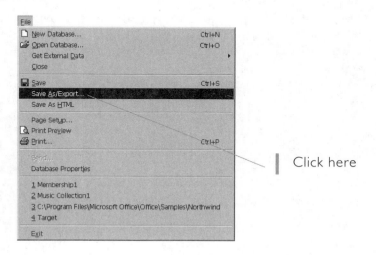

Click here

Access 97 users can export reports into HTML format and then publish them on the World Wide Web.

To do this, follow the procedures on page 34.

2 Click here

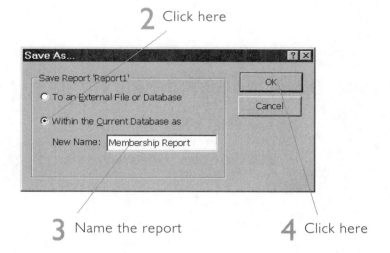

3 Name the report

4 Click here

Opening/closing reports

When you open a report you've previously saved to disk, Access displays it in Print Preview mode. (Note, however, that when you create a new report with the Report Wizard or with AutoReport, by default Access previews it automatically – see earlier topics for more information on this.)

You can't edit reports in Print Preview mode: you can only inspect them.

Opening a report

First, ensure the Database window is visible (for how to do this, see page 37 in Chapter 3). Now do the following:

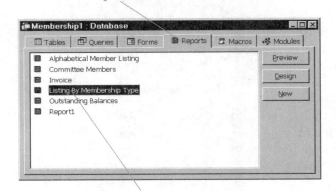

Activate the Reports tab

2 Double-click the report you want to view

Closing down a report

Do the following:

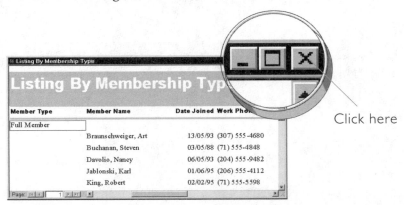

Click here

Creating graphs

This chapter shows you how to view your data graphically, as a chart. You'll learn to create charts either as separate forms or reports in their own right, or as part of existing forms/reports. You'll learn how to specify the chart type, either during the process of creation or subsequently. You'll also discover how to launch Microsoft Graph to modify the underlying data or format of your graphs in a variety of ways.

Covers

Chapter Eight

Graphs – an overview

Graphs give your data visual impact, and make it more assimilable. They also:

- reveal hidden relationships between data

- make trends much more apparent

In one sense, graphs are similar to forms and reports: they let you view your data in a highly specific – and useful – fashion.

Graph creation

You create graphs in Access with the help of the Graph Wizard. You can use this wizard in two ways:

- when you create a special form or report from scratch

- from within existing forms or reports, in Design View

The first method is the easiest and quickest way to create a new graph. When you create a graph in this way, Access builds a new form or report with a single graph in it.

Access 95 lets you create graphs in Form Design and Report Design mode.

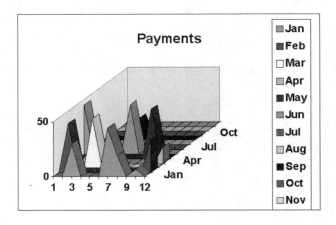

A new graph, excerpted from a form

When you use the second method, however, the result is identical with one exception: you can choose to link the graph to fields in the form/report.

Creating a graph from scratch (1)

First, ensure the Database window is visible (for how to do this, see Chapter 3). Then carry out the following steps:

Activate either of these tabs

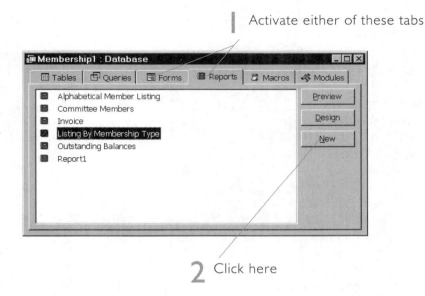

2 Click here

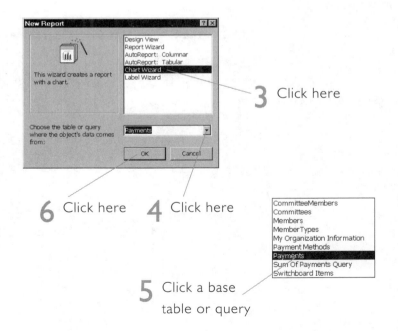

3 Click here

6 Click here   4 Click here

5 Click a base table or query

Creating a graph from scratch (2)

Now carry out the following steps:

1 Double-click the fields you want to include

At least one of the fields you select must contain numerical data (e.g. – as here – currency information).

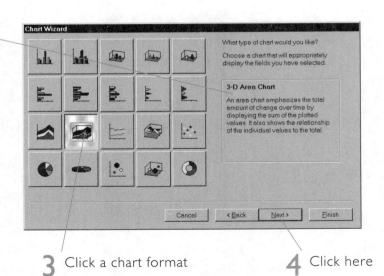

Access provides a potted description of each chart type here:

2 Click here

In Access 95, this dialog offers fewer available chart types.

3 Click a chart format

4 Click here

Creating a graph from scratch (3)

In the next dialog, Access displays the selected fields as buttons. It makes certain assumptions about which axes the fields should occupy, and displays a brief illustration of the result on the left of the dialog. If you want to change these assumptions, carry out steps 1-2 below, then follow step 3. If you don't, simply follow step 3:

1 Click and hold on a field button . . .

HANDY TIP

Re step 2 – when you drag the field button, the cursor changes. (See the magnified section in the dialog.)

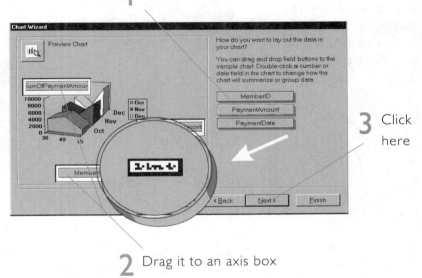

3 Click here

2 Drag it to an axis box

Previewing your chart...

Before you proceed, you can inspect how your chart looks. Click the Preview Chart button: in the top left hand corner of the above dialog. This is the result:

HANDY TIP

To close the Preview window and continue with the Chart Wizard, press Esc. Follow step 3 above to move on to the next stage...

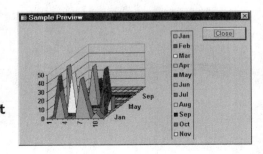

Creating a graph from scratch (4)

Carry out the final steps below:

 REMEMBER

The Chart Wizard assumes you want a 'legend' (text which links chart colours with the data they represent) included in the chart. If you don't, click here *before* step 3.

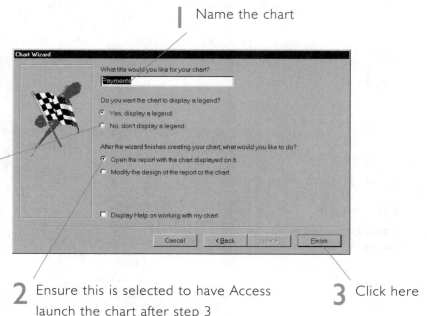

1 Name the chart

2 Ensure this is selected to have Access launch the chart after step 3

3 Click here

This is the final result (in this instance, Access has opened the report which contains the new chart):

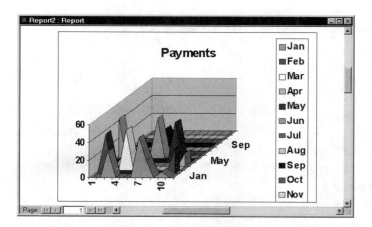

Creating an in-line graph (1)

You can also run the Graph Wizard from within an existing form or report; however, the launch procedure is different.

The example discussed in this and subsequent topics shows the addition of a graph to an existing form; the procedure is essentially the same for a report...

First, open the relevant form or report (for how to do this, see the appropriate topics in Chapters 4 and 7 respectively). Then pull down the View menu and click Design View. (In Access 95, however, click Form Design or Report Design, as appropriate.) Finally, pull down the Insert menu and do the following:

In Access 95, the Insert menu is slightly different.

Click here

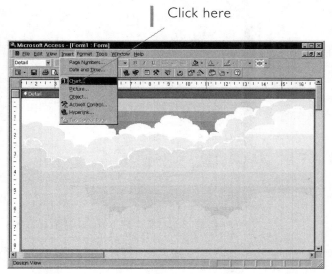

The mouse cursor changes:

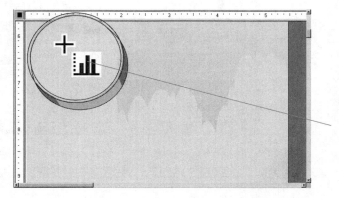

Magnified view of cursor

Creating an in-line graph (2)

Position the transformed cursor at the point where you want the chart to begin. Press and hold down the left mouse button; drag to define the chart area:

Defined chart area

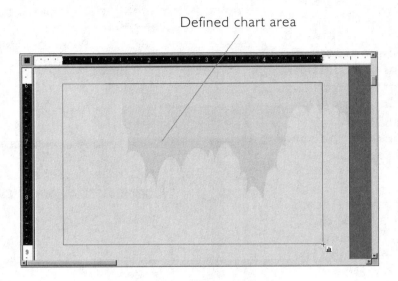

When you release the mouse button, the dialog below launches. Carry out the following steps:

2 Click a table or query

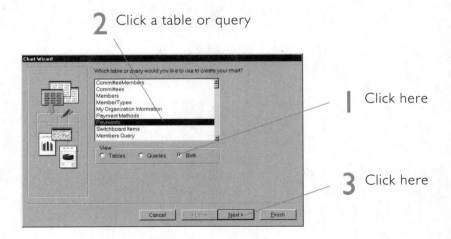

Click here

3 Click here

Creating an in-line graph (3)

Complete the following steps:

1 Double-click the field(s) you want to include

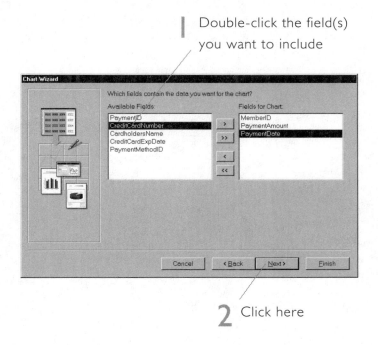

2 Click here

In Access 95, this dialog offers fewer available chart formats.

3 Click a chart format

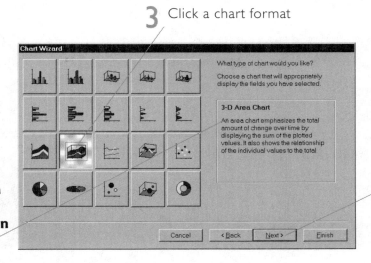

Access provides a potted description of the selected format here:

4 Click here

Creating an in-line graph (4)

Now, Access displays the selected fields as buttons and makes certain assumptions about which axes the fields should occupy. If you want to change these assumptions, carry out steps 1-2 below, then follow step 3. If you don't, simply follow step 3:

1 Click and hold on a field button...

Re step 2 – when you drag the field button, the cursor changes. (See the magnified section in the dialog.)

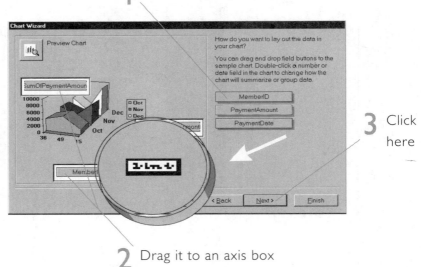

3 Click here

2 Drag it to an axis box

If you want to link the data in your graph with fields in the underlying form or report, do the following:

If you don't want to link any fields, simply carry out step 6.

4 Click here; select a field in the list

5 Click here; select a field in the list

6 Click here

Creating an in-line graph (5)

Carry out the final steps below:

HANDY TIP The Chart Wizard assumes you want a 'legend' (text which links chart colours with the data they represent) included in the chart. If you don't, click here *before* step 2.

1 | Name the chart

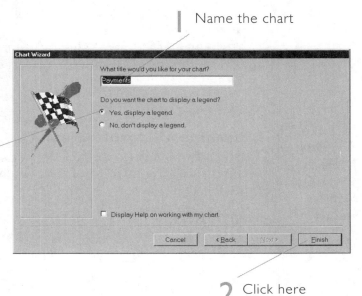

2 | Click here

This is the final result (in this instance, Access has inserted the new chart into the original form):

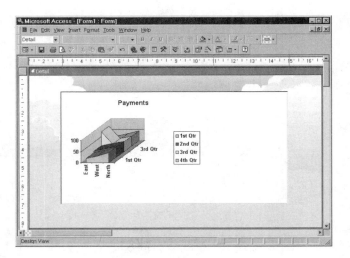

Amending graphs (1)

However you use the Graph Wizard (either in the creation of a new form/report or from within an existing form/report), what actually happens is that Access launches a separate program – Microsoft Graph – behind the scenes. With the use of a kind of sleight of hand, Graph creates the chart and inserts it seamlessly into your form or report.

To modify existing charts, however, you have to make Microsoft Graph visible.

REMEMBER **In Access 95, Design View is known as Form Design or Report Design mode.**

Launching Microsoft Graph (1)

This is a two-stage process. The first stage is to launch (in Design View) the form or report which contains the chart you want to alter.

Make sure the Database window is visible (for how to do this, see page 37 in Chapter 3). Then do the following:

Activate either of these tabs

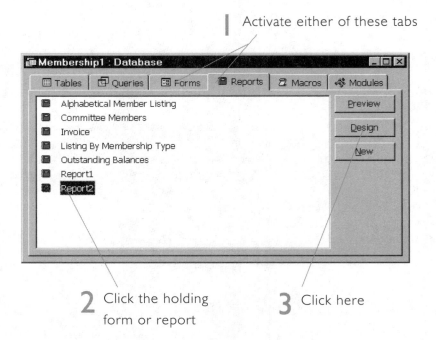

2 Click the holding form or report

3 Click here

Amending graphs (2)

Launching Microsoft Graph (2)

In the second stage, do the following:

Here, the chart is shown after a *single* click, for illustration purposes.

Double-click anywhere in the chart area

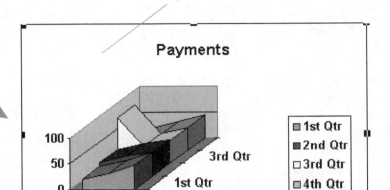

This is the result:

Datasheet window

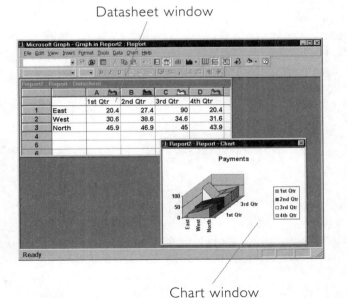

Microsoft Graph

Chart window

Amending graphs (3)

Microsoft Graph consists of two components (click either component to activate it):

- the Datasheet window

- the Chart window

You can use the Datasheet window to enter/amend data; it works as a mini-table (see Chapter 3 for how to use it).

You can use the Chart window to:

Re point 1 – Access 95 users should click Chart Type in the *Format* menu. Then follow the remaining instructions.

1. Amend the chart type

Pull down the Chart menu and click Chart Type. Select a new type in the Chart Type dialog and click OK to apply it

Re point 2 – Access 95 users need to apply an AutoFormat instead of a custom format.
  Pull down the Format menu and click AutoFormat. Select a Gallery – chart type – and then a sub-type. Click OK.

2. Apply a custom format

Pull down the Chart menu and click Chart Type. Click the Custom Types tab. Select a chart type. Click OK to apply it

3. Change the typeface and/or type size for legends

Select the text by clicking it. Pull down the Format menu and click Font. In the dialog, click a new font or size. Click OK to apply your changes

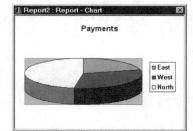

The original chart with its chart type changed to 3-D Pie

To save your finished graph to disk, follow the Save procedures outlined in Chapters 4 (Forms) and 7 (Reports).

When you've finished working in Graph, pull down the File menu and click Exit & Return to ... (the ellipsis denotes text which changes according to whether the graph is contained in a form or report). You're returned to Access, and the original chart is automatically updated.

Printing your data

This chapter shows you how to print out your data. Before you do this, however, you'll learn how to ensure that the overall page layout is correct. You'll discover how to revise margin settings; allocate a page size/orientation; and – in the case of forms and reports – specify column dimensions. You'll go on to preview your work, using the Access Print Preview window, before finally customising print settings and printing your data.

Covers

Chapter Nine

Printing – an overview

Access handles printing in broadly the same way, irrespective of whether you're printing tables, forms, reports or queries.

In spite of this, however, there are differences:

- tables and queries have fewer incidental criteria you can set before you begin a print-run (the available settings are limited to margins and page size/orientation)

- with forms and reports, you can set a variety of additional layout and page setup criteria (principally relating to multi-column documents) before you begin printing

In spite of these discrepancies, you can always preview your work before you commit yourself to printing it. This is advisable because:

- the Access Print Preview screen provides a fully WYSIWYG (What You See Is What You Get) representation of what your data will look like when printed

- Access data (especially in tables) frequently spreads across more than one page; Print Preview gives you a bird's-eye view of this process in operation

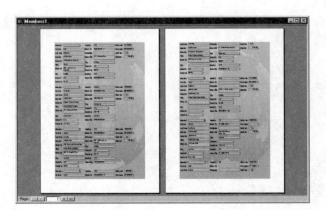

A form
in Print
Preview

Page Setup issues (1)

If you intend to print tables, queries, forms or reports, you need to ensure that the correct page setup/layout criteria are in force before you do so.

First, ensure the Database window is open (for how to do this, see page 37). Carry out the following steps:

Activate one of these tabs

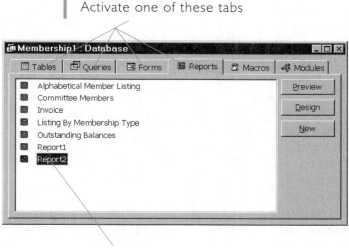

2 Double-click a table, query, form or report

The selected database component is opened. Now pull down the File menu and do the following:

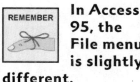

In Access 95, the File menu is slightly different.

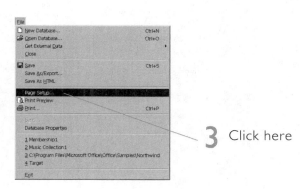

3 Click here

Page Setup issues (2)

Setting margin sizes

Follow the procedures on page 145 then do the following:

Ensure this tab is active

In tables, this option is Print Headings. Deselect it if you don't want column headings to print.

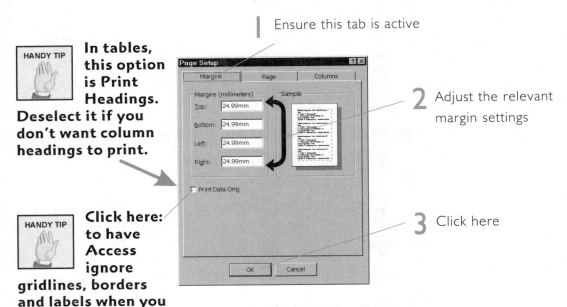

2 Adjust the relevant margin settings

Click here: to have Access ignore gridlines, borders and labels when you begin the print-run.

3 Click here

Setting page size/orientation

Follow the procedures on page 145. Carry out step 1 below, then 2 and/or 3, as appropriate. Finally, follow step 4:

Re step 2 – see the following for details of orientation types:

Activate this tab

Portrait

Landscape

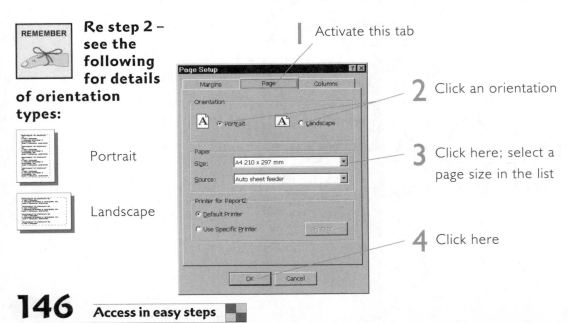

2 Click an orientation

3 Click here; select a page size in the list

4 Click here

Page Setup issues (3)

Specifying column layouts

In forms or reports, you can determine:

- how many columns data prints in
- the gap between rows
- the inter-column spacing
- the column width and/or height
- the order in which Access prints fields within records

Follow the procedure on page 145 then carry out step 1 below. Follow steps 2-5, as appropriate, then step 6:

Re step 1 – Access 95 users should click the Layout tab. Additionally, the dialog itself is slightly different...

Click the relevant option here to determine print direction:

 Down, then Across

 Across, then Down

Finally, follow step 6.

2 Type in the number of columns

1 Activate this tab

3 Type in a row spacing

4 Type in a column gap

5 Insert a column width and/or row height

6 Click here

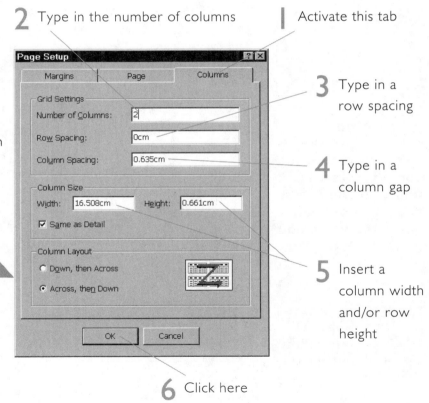

Launching Print Preview

You can preview any database component before printing it.

First, launch the Database window (see page 37 for how to do this). Then carry out the following steps.

Activate one of these tabs

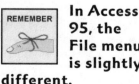

HANDY TIP

You can also preview database components after you've opened them. Simply pull down the File menu and follow step 3.

2 Click the table, query, form or report you want to preview

Now pull down the File menu and do the following:

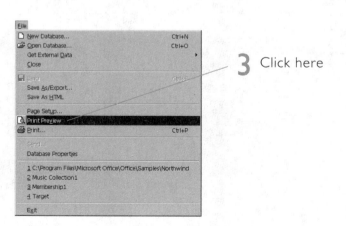

3 Click here

REMEMBER

In Access 95, the File menu is slightly different.

Using Print Preview (1)

When you opt to preview a database component, Access launches a special Print Preview window showing how the component will look when printed:

Print Preview toolbar

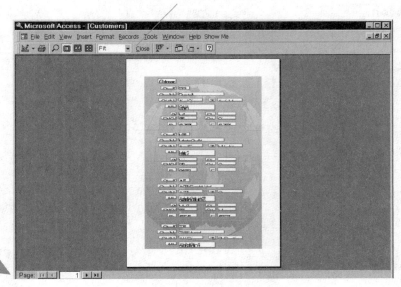

REMEMBER **These are the Print Preview navigation controls. See page 152 for how to use them.**

The Print Preview window has its own dedicated toolbar (see above). You can use this to:

• zoom in or out (there are two methods)

• apply a preset Zoom percentage (e.g. 150%, 200%)

• specify the view spread (1 or 2 pages)

• initiate printing immediately

You can also use the navigation controls in the bottom left-hand corner of the Print Preview window to (among other things) move to a precise page instantly.

Using Print Preview (2)

Zooming in and out (1)

Access 95 users should click this button:

in the Print Preview toolbar.

Refer to the Print Preview toolbar and do the following:

Click here

to alternate between:

*   Full Page view (where the whole page is visible in the Print Preview window); and

REMEMBER

In Access 95, the Print Preview toolbar is somewhat different.

*   whichever Zoom level was previously set (see the 'Using Print Preview (3)' topic)

Zooming in and out (2)

You can also use a variation on the above technique to select which area of the database component you want to zoom in on.

Carry out the above procedure, then position the mouse pointer over the section of the Print Preview window you want to magnify – the cursor becomes a magnifying glass:

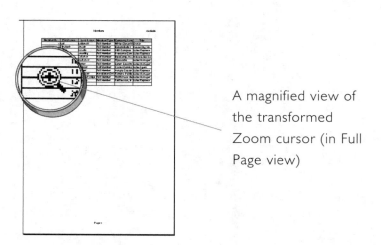

A magnified view of the transformed Zoom cursor (in Full Page view)

Left-click once to zoom in; click again to revert to Full Page view.

Using Print Preview (3)

Applying a preset Zoom percentage

Refer to the Print Preview toolbar and do the following:

To specify your own Zoom %, instead of following step 2 type in a % here: then press Enter.

Click here

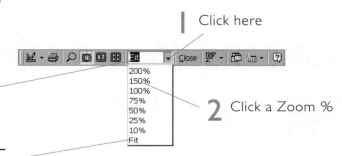

200%
150%
100%
75%
50%
25%
10%
Fit

2 Click a Zoom %

Re step 2 – click Fit to have Access choose a Zoom level which displays your table, query, form or report optimally, according to the size of the window.

Specifying the view spread

Refer to the Print Preview toolbar and do the following:

Click here to view a single page

Click here to view two pages

In Access 95, the Print Preview toolbar is somewhat different.

A one-page spread

A two-page spread

Using Print Preview (4)

Initiating a print-run
If you know that the relevant print criteria are correctly set (see pages 153 and 154 for how to set these), you can use the Print Preview toolbar to have Access start printing your data *immediately*, without launching the Print dialog.

 In Access 95, the Print Preview toolbar is somewhat different.

Do the following:

Click here

Using the navigation controls
You can use the navigation controls in the bottom left-hand corner of the Print Preview window to jump to:

- a specific page

- the previous page

- the next page

- the first page

- the last page

 To close the Print Preview window, simply press Esc. Or click:

in the Print Preview toolbar.

Click where indicated below (or to move to a specific page, enter the page number):

To the first page   Type in a page number and press Enter   To the last page

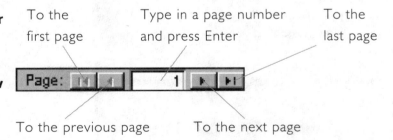

To the previous page   To the next page

Printing your data (1)

Printing is a two-stage process.

Preparing to print

First, preview the database component you want to print (for how to do this, see the 'Launching Print Preview' and 'Using Print Preview' topics earlier). Close the Print Preview window and launch the Database window (see page 37 for how to do this). Then do the following:

Activate one of these tabs

2 Double-click a table, query, form or report

The selected database component is opened. Now pull down the File menu and do the following:

If you opened a form or table in step 2 and only want to print specific records, select them *before* you follow step 3.

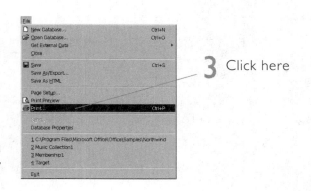

3 Click here

In Access 95, the File menu is slightly different.

Printing your data (2)

Setting the print criteria

You can:

- specify the printer you want to use

- print the whole database component (the default)

- print a specific page range (e.g. pages 10-15)

- confine the print run to records you selected earlier

- specify the number of copies printed

- turn collation off or on. Collation is the process whereby Access prints one full copy at a time. For instance, if you're printing 5 copies of a 12-page database, when collation is active Access prints pages 1-12 of the first copy, 1-12 of the second copy, and so on...

Carry out any of steps 1-5 below. Finally, follow step 6:

In Access 95, the Print dialog is somewhat different.

If you need to adjust your printer settings, click here: *before* **carrying out step 6.**
(See your printer's manual for how to complete the resulting dialogs.)

1 Click here; select a printer in the list

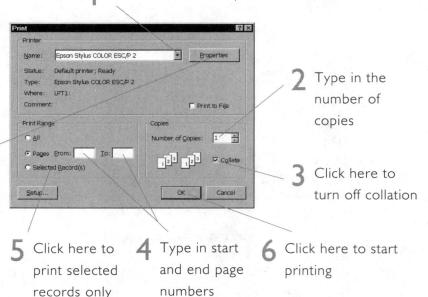

2 Type in the number of copies

3 Click here to turn off collation

5 Click here to print selected records only

4 Type in start and end page numbers

6 Click here to start printing

Index